POSEIDON PRESS

New York

London

Toronto

Sydney

Tokyo

Singapore

He suggested to Adams, who wanted to make a position for himself, that an article . . . would attract as much attention, and probably break as much glass, as any other stone that could be thrown by a beginner.

The Education of Henry Adams

CONTENTS

Introduction

Tom Wolfe

As Bruce Bawer says in these pages, no generation in history has ever been more lavishly analyzed, dramatized, mythologized, and agonized over than the Baby Boomers, the Americans who were born between 1946 and 1964. The Boomers' boom was a boom in the birth rate following the Depression and the Second World War. But these children also grew up during perhaps the greatest economic boom any major nation has ever experienced and during a time when the United States swelled up into one of the two giants who trod the globe. From amidst all these booms and heavy footfalls emerged such fabled babies as the hippies, the New Left, the Vietnam Generation, the Jesus People, the New Agers, and the yuppies.

In my opinion, myth is not too pompous a word for the aura that shone 'round about them. For a time they were seen as completely new creatures in the history of evolution. One of the foundations of Marshall McLuhan's communications theory was his belief that heavy exposure to television had altered, literally altered, the Baby Boomers' "sensory balance." He was talking about the relative importance of their senses of hearing, seeing, tasting, smelling, and touching. For reasons that needn't detain us here, McLuhan thought it was not the sense of sight but the sense of touch that TV engorged and enlarged. To him, this explained another boom boom boom of the Boomers' youth, namely, the sexual revolution.

Jean-François Revel made a tour of American college campuses at the height of the New Left and hippie or psychedelic movements of the late 1960s and wrote a book entitled *Without Marx or Jesus* in which he said that in the United States had arisen a new man. *Homo novus* he called this creature, as if only Latin could adequately capture the evolutionary importance of the phenomenon. *Homo novus* had a utopian vision which was neither Marx's vision nor Jesus's but an entirely new one. Many of the popular ideas on the campuses seemed to be Marxist, Revel said, but on close inspection they turned out to be sentiments floating fuzzily in "a Marxist mist." For example, on the campuses *humani novi* often said that the dark night of fascism was descending upon America. Here, said Revel, was one of the great mysteries of astronomy. The dark night of fascism was forever descending upon America, but it touched ground only in Europe.

Revel's sense of irony saved him from going utterly overboard. But Charles Reich's passion for *homo novus* was unconditional. Reich, who is recalled for us herein by Richard Brookhiser, wrote a book entitled *The Greening of America*. For about twenty months it was hailed as a *Social Contract* for the twentieth century. Reich's true literary ancestor, however, was not Rousseau but Matthew Arnold. Arnold, who gave us the terms "culture," meaning the arts, "philistine," meaning someone who doesn't get it in the arts, and "commuter," meaning a philistine who works in the city but lives outside it, was another believer in rapid changes in human evolution. A hundred years ago, in his analysis, a new creature had arisen. In addition to the traditional upper classes, which he called "the Barbarians," and the middle classes, which he called "the Philistines," and the lower classes, which he called "the Populace"—even in the nineteenth century intellectuals didn't dare give the lower orders funny names—there was a new class that was now visible, gliding above the old order. These were "the people of sweetness and light." "Sweetness and light" was another Arnold coinage. It was not at all ironic. The people of sweetness and light were the same as Coleridge's "clerisy" of fifty years earlier, who, said Coleridge, had replaced the clergy as the creators of moral values. And he was right. Today we use the simpler term "intellectuals." To Reich *homo novus baby boomis* had far more than a superior intellect. The *novus* one also had more profound feelings, an exquisitely richer sensory and emotional appreciation of the world and its possibilities. What America was greening into, thanks to the young, was an Eden of lofty sentiments.

That being the case, it was time for the old to learn from the young. One result of this notion was a new kind of drama in which the heroes and heroines are young people, who possess superior knowledge and feelings, and the old either learn from them or look ridiculous and backward. Bawer mentions *The Graduate* and *Easy Rider* as the first in a long line of movies of this sort. As a footnote, I would add *Dirty Dancing*. At the end of *Dirty Dancing*, the middle-aged paying customers at a resort hotel realize the errors of their osteoporotic ways and join the teenage kitchen and maid-service help in an orgy of groin-socketed lambada . . . as we fade out. . . .

There was, indeed, something entirely new about the boomers, although it had nothing to do with human evolution. They grew up at a time when there was so much fat in the American economy that people in their teens and early twenties could lay hands on enough money to create styles of life all their own. I first noticed this among the surfers of Southern California. Surfers were not merely athletes but people who in many cases were able to live communally, in apartments and abandoned buildings, in the same towns as their parents, for days, weeks, sometimes months at a time. In the same fashion, the hippies, the New Lefters, the Jesus People, the New Agers—all were able to live communally at young ages and to develop distinctive codes of dress and decor (and language) and thereby to create styles of life in precisely the sense that Max Weber originally intended that term.

The money came from home—many hippies and New Lefters were remittance men—and it came from the government in the form of welfare and entitlements, to use the going word. One way or another, it was inhaled from the breathtaking surpluses of the economic boom which began about 1943 and which, despite the heavy weather of the year 1990, has not ended yet.

Which brings us, finally, to the yuppies. All of the contributors to this volume are of yuppie age. So naturally many of them, such as Maggie Gallagher, George Sim Johnston, and Richard Vigilante, are concerned with the validity, or lack of it, of the yuppie tag. In a marvelously funny piece called "House Lust," Maggie Gallagher says that most boomers, far from moving up financially, are sliding downward. Eventually, she says, "you come to realize that you will never again achieve the standard of living you had in junior high school," when you lived on a lovely, leafy plot of ground in your own house. Nevertheless, the money fever remains, and that is what creates the very nearly sensual lust for a house that "House Lust" so lovingly describes. At the heart of the yuppie life—and *yuppie* was, whether we like it or not, *the* social term to come out of the 1980s—was not the acquisition of money but the lust for money and, above all, the kind of public display that money makes possible. In my opinion not many boomers want to be plutocrats. A plutocrat is one who rules through money. That is not a boomer's aspiration, as David Brooks demonstrates quite deftly in his confessions of a Washington "policy wonk." But Brooks's wonderful wonk does have well-developed plutographic instincts. The plutographer is one who merely wants to live a life that *looks like*, that graphically depicts, the life of the plutocrat, without any of the plutocrat's responsibilities. Hence the most famous of the yuppie passions, the passion to be seen at this week's restaurant of the century.

At bottom, the yuppie is not terribly different from the

hippie or the New Lefter. Each has taken a good deep whiff of the surplus wealth of the American economy (to draw from the vocabulary of those late twentieth-century reactionaries, the Marxists) and decided to use it to create a life few young people have ever dared live before. The yuppies' problem is that they have no Aldous Huxleys, Reichs, or Marcuses to adorn them with wreaths of moral and intellectual respectability.

Maggie Gallagher and Richard Vigilante would probably quarrel even with the credence I've given the term yuppie in the last two paragraphs. And that would be fine by me. One of the most engaging things about the fifteen writers in this volume is their refusal to accept clichés and conventional wisdom. The picture they give us of their own breed, the baby boomers, comes not from out of the heat of politics or the money fever. It is the view in the dawn of the morning after. In this book the boomers are still onstage. They still enjoy talking about themselves. In fact, they love it. But they have just taken a cold shower. And their thoughts are very clear, albeit with a trace of a headache, and bracing and full of the wit of those who are still young enough to be exuberant and world-weary at the same time.

Foreword

Terry Teachout

"*I*t occurs to me," says Arthur Winner, the fifty-four-year-old small-town lawyer and WASP ascendant who is the hero of James Gould Cozzens's 1957 novel *By Love Possessed*, "that youth's a kind of infirmity. You don't have the use of your logical faculties—or, at least, most of us don't." I wonder what Arthur Winner would have had to say about the infirmities of youth in 1968, the year he turned sixty-five. That was the year when Bobby Kennedy and Martin Luther King, Jr., were assassinated; when the Chicago Seven trashed the Democratic Presidential convention and thereby put Richard Nixon in the White House; when the children of the '60s took over the asylum and gleefully unlocked all the padded cells. "Sgt. Pepper's Lonely Hearts Club Band" was a year in the past, Woodstock a year in the future. It was the exemplary year of an exemplary decade, if you have a taste for cautionary tales.

Arthur Winner would be eighty-seven years old as I write, not an implausible age for a New England WASP of good stock to attain, assuming that the events of 1968 didn't bring about his early demise. He would know from reading *Time* and *Newsweek* that the baby boomers, those Americans born between 1946 and 1964 and subsequently much beloved of magazine editors and talk show hosts, have now assumed positions of political and cultural power in American life. He would also know, doubtless to his surprise and delight, that they didn't turn out quite as expected.

Journalistic pundits are still accustomed to viewing the baby boomers in the lurid light of the '60s. To them, the boomers are bearded, dope-smoking Deadheads who, grown up at last, are exercising their newfound power in terms of the values of their revolutionary youth. To be sure, there are more than a few such people kicking around in America today, and these people, the baby boomers who came of age in the '60s, continue to fascinate the media. But the baby boom generation is far more complicated than that. The boomers who came of age in the '70s, for example, put Ronald Reagan in the White House and show no apparent signs of regret over having done so. A recent *New York Times/ CBS News* poll on party affiliation showed that 43% of Americans between the ages of thirty and forty-four consider themselves Republicans, as do 45% of Americans between the ages of eighteen and twenty-nine. Given the obvious fact that there are more "conservative" Democrats than "liberal" Republicans, it begins to look as if something new and drastically different is happening—and that "Mr. Jones," the Arthur Winner-type establishment pillar of Bob Dylan's "Ballad of a Thin Man," who had read all of F. Scott Fitzgerald's books but somehow couldn't figure out the '60s, still doesn't know what it is.

The cultural and political stereotypes that define the place of the baby boomers in American life are, in other words, somewhat wide of the mark. Most baby boomers, it turns out, are politically and culturally right of center, albeit in idiosyncratic and often unpredictable ways. This is especially true of those born during the second half of the boom, the ones too young to have served in Vietnam and thus untouched by the wrenching, disabling agonies of the war. Everybody expected the older baby boomers to reshape America in their famously scruffy image. It never happened. In fact, their younger brothers and sisters have already done far more to change the way we live now. It's the younger boomers who are manning the desks in Washington, D.C.; who are wielding steadily increasing influence in corporate boardrooms and TV control rooms; who, as they reach their mid-thirties, are firmly grasping the levers of power that the older boomers relinquished when Richard Nixon went home to California and America got out of Vietnam.

If you happened to be in New York on the first Wednesday of any given month, you could look in on a group of younger baby boomers who are helping to change the way America votes and thinks and lives. We call ourselves the Vile Body. We meet once a month in the library of a borrowed townhouse on the Upper East Side, where we drink, eat stale popcorn and pretzels, and talk endlessly and informally about whatever happens to be on our minds. We live in and around New York, though you can usually find a few visiting firemen from Washington. We range in age from twenty-five to thirtysomething. We work on Wall Street and at major corporations, for newspapers and magazines and publishing houses and think tanks; we are busy writing our first books, starting up our first companies, making our first movies, raising our first children.

Like most people our age, we voted for Ronald Reagan and, later, George Bush. Many of us (though by no means all) call ourselves "conservatives." But comparatively few of the people you're likely to see at the Vile Body accept the ideological package deal of the conservative movement without significant reservations here and there. Like the rest of our fellow boomers, we wander all over the map when it comes to abortion, sexual morality, foreign policy, cultural matters. Some of us are traditional conservatives, others radical libertarians. Some of us like to watch "Yo! MTV Raps," others prefer to commune with Mozart and Verdi. Some of us are orthodox Catholics, some secular Jews, some staunch atheists. The only thing on which you can be sure all of us agree is this: that the political and intellectual legacies of our older brothers and sisters, the baby boomers of the '60s, were a flop, a failure, a disaster.

We represent the vast majority of baby boomers, the ones who gladly put the '60s behind them without a second thought. The purpose of this book is to allow you to meet a few of us and hear what we have to say. We've put our thoughts into a book because you won't find them on the op-ed page of your local newspaper. Not yet, anyway. Most of the voices you're likely to encounter there belong to exhausted liberals, middle-aged conservatives, and bitter, confused victims of the worst excesses of the '60s. These people, even the best of them, belong to the past. This book is about tomorrow—and the day after tomorrow.

Most of the contributors to this book are friends; most of us attend the Vile Body fairly regularly. The oldest contributor was born in 1951, the youngest in 1961. Our average age is thirty-three. All but four of us live and work in the New York area. Three hail from Washington; the fourth, a native New Yorker, now lives in Brussels. We come from big Eastern cities and small Midwestern towns. We went to Yale, Harvard, the University of Chicago, Berkeley, and all points in between. None of the men among us served in Vietnam; only one was old enough for it to have been a realistic possibility.

Only three of us hold graduate degrees in anything, for we have chosen, in some cases against natural inclination, to make our way outside the academy, which in recent years has turned into a thoroughly uncongenial intellectual retirement home for tenured radicals of the '60s. We are yuppies, most of us and more or less, but none of us is a Master of the Universe. Instead, we are all certified members of what Joseph Epstein has called the "verbal class," and we support our middle-class life-styles, sometimes tenuously, by writing books and essays and poetry and editorials about everything under the sun: party politics, tort liability, deconstructionism, radical feminism, the latest movies, the New York dance scene.

Thirteen of us work or have worked on the staffs of magazines ranging from *National Review* and *The New Criterion* to *Harper's* and *U.S. News and World Report*. One has just started a magazine of his own. Four are presently employed by major newspapers or newspaper chains. Three work for think tanks. Two are full-time critics. One is a Wall Street executive who quit his job to write a novel. One spent the better part of a year in Afghanistan covering the war there. One is a "Jeopardy!" champion. One teaches piano, another used to play jazz in Kansas City bars and nightclubs. Nine of us are married, two to each other; one is a single mother. We have produced five children (four more are in the works) and have collectively published or are on the verge of publishing fourteen books, counting this one.

What we think is as diverse as who we are. The book you hold in your hands is not a monolithic manifesto, an *I'll Take My Stand* for the David Letterman generation. It contains, by design but without contrivance, a very wide range of opinion on a very wide range of subjects. You will find contributors who contradict each other as aggressively in the pages of this book as they do over drinks at the Vile Body. Some of these essays are frankly autobiographical in tone, others coolly detached. Some are funny, others deadly serious. You will find in this book the same diversity of opinion that you would encounter if you put fifteen representative baby boomers in a small room and told them to have at it.

What you won't find here is what you are used to finding whenever you see the dread words "baby boomer" in print. This book contains no stale '60s romanticism, no wan '70s disillusion, no tedious '80s whining. It isn't about what you think you already know about us. It's about what you don't know about us. It will tell you what our generation really thinks about politics and religion, art and culture, sex and drugs, marriage and family. It is, in short, a book about the '90s. If you want to find out what the '90s are going to be like, turn the page.

The Great Baby Boom Bust

Richard Brookhiser

T he Old Campus of Yale is a large quadrangle ringed by brooding brownstone sort-of Gothic dormitories in which the college stores its freshmen. In the spring of 1975, much of it was torn up by excavations, whether to repair the century-old drainage system or to plant replacements for the dying elm trees I do not now remember, and the excavation sites were lined with plank walls. The mild spring night that Saigon fell, these walls became covered with jubilant graffiti celebrating the end of American imperialism, the dawn of Vietnamese liberty, and kindred events. These sentiments striking a few of us as mistaken, we bought some cans of white paint and some brushes and went out later that night, not to paint up pro-imperialist, anti-liberty slogans of our own, but simply to efface the slogans that were already there. We had got halfway through the work of whiteout when the original authors appeared. Words were exchanged, then shoves, then the would-be future leaders of America tried pouring paint over each other's heads. I happened to see one of my antagonists at a distance still later that evening. He had not changed his jeans, which were faintly luminous. He was still excited by our political encounter and threw jerky go-team punches at the night air as he strode along. I had lost a pair of shoes. Several hundred thousand Vietnamese would lose their lives.

Most of my fellow Yalies, I am pretty sure, would not have approved of the first set of slogans in all their vehemence. Certainly they would not have approved of taking the trouble to write them up publicly (this was, after all, the mid-'70s). But the underlying analysis was familiar, and generally accepted. Thieu was a tyrant; Nixon had been unmasked as a criminal; for years, America had been dealing death to Asians and anxiety to draft-age college students. The sooner the last threads of involvement were cut, the better. The anti-sloganeers would have been considered not only impassioned, and hence eccentric, but wrong.

Nine and a half years later, I was on a different campus for a different kind of occasion. President Ronald Reagan, in the homestretch of the 1984 election, was making the next-to-last campaign swing of his life. The only serious political question left at that stage was whether Walter Mondale's tally of electoral votes would break into double digits. Reagan was making an appearance in the basketball auditorium at Ohio State, a Mussolini *moderne* structure that looks like a set of replicas of the Hirschhorn Gallery stacked one on top of the other. The ascending circular stands were packed with students, and they yelled like hell. I was with the fourth estate, down at floor level. The fourth estate always has a little roped-off section to itself at these events. It's supposed to guarantee our sight lines; it makes it easier to herd us in and out; and it fosters that indispensable sense of fourth-estate camaraderie: *us* judging *them*. Sometimes the section is off to the side of the crowd; sometimes it is behind (for seeing over *their* heads). That afternoon, the fourth estate was at the bottom of this monumental column of sound, and we all looked a little—uncomfortable. Volunteers from the Ohio State Marching Band were supplying the music, a sonic steam-roller, and that no doubt helped to work the crowd up. Woody Hayes was on the platform, as the gods sometimes mingle with mortals, and that helped, too. The Reagan advance men, finally, had been leading the crowd in wave cheers, in which a shout passes around an auditorium section by section, at the speed of a slow searchlight, two or three times, and then everyone lets loose together. So that the sound was not just falling on the heads of the fourth estate, but rolling around up there like an air raid before it finally cascaded down.

But the big draw, the authentic thrill for this crowd, was Reagan himself. And not just for Reagan the performer, though he handled the crowd perfectly, the perfection consisting in the way he had then, at the peak of his skills, of not seeming to handle them at all. When he first appeared on the podium, and the decibel level jumped up another notch, and the fourth estate gave an extra little wince, it was several moments, as he moved down the platform, deferentially shaking hands, before he even seemed to notice and acknowledge that he was the cause of this grotesque uproar: *Gee, aren't all these people here to see former Governor Bricker?* No, the crowd also liked what he said. Reagan gave his standard stump speech, which they interrupted twenty, thirty times for whoops: taxes—*boo;* U.S.A.—*yay*—and on and on. But the line they liked best, these young throats, who had been in third and fourth and fifth grade nine and a half years ago, came in a reference to Grenada, and it was that, during Reagan's first term, "not one square inch" of territory had been lost to "Communist aggression." Two-minute standing ovation. Tell that to the sign painters.

The handiest definition of the baby boom is the generation born between 1946 and 1964, the years that mark the plateau of the postwar birthrate. Pat Caddell, the Democratic pollster, would put the cutoff at 1960 and shove the starting date back as well. Another way of defining the first measure is: all the children, from eldest to youngest, of men who fought, or might have fought, in World War II and Korea. Another way of putting Caddell's measure is: everyone who was in high school or college, if they went to college, at some point during that fifteen-year decade of the Greater '60s that began with JFK moving into the

White House and ended with the last helicopter lifting off from the American embassy to South Vietnam. By either definition, the cast of characters in my first memory were boomers, albeit tail-end, while the crowd providing the foreground noise of the second belonged to the next wave, whatever that comes to be called. The contrast between the two has been the stuff of pondering by experts for years. What does the boom generation want, and how will it vote? Do their juniors want something else? Has the boom generation itself changed as it has grown older? Is there a magic key to any or all of these generations? If someone has it, how do we sign him up?

Like rummies in an OTB parlor, or guests at a Predators' Ball, the experts have bet a lot on both generations. The boom generation has drawn the most action because it is bigger—the American birthrate began to dip in the '60s—hence, the potential rewards for figuring out its desires are greater.

The earliest investors in boom stock expected nothing less than the end of life as we know it. It may be cruel to quote Charles Reich at this late date; there were those who thought it was cruel to quote him in his heyday. But lots of people bought *The Greening of America*. George McGovern gave it a blurb. Indeed, Reich was half of a two-man Golden Age of the Yale faculty, his fellow professor and best-selling writer being Erich Segal, classicist and author of *Love Story*. "There is a revolution coming," Reich wrote, ". . . the revolution of a new generation. Their protest and rebellion, their culture, clothes, music, drugs, ways of thought, and liberated life-style are not a passing fad." Their task was "to be the teachers of their fellow men and women, so that the great liberating process of recovery of self, started by our youth, can become the means of liberation for all Americans. . . . When self is recovered, the power of the Corporate State will be ended, as miraculously as a kiss breaks a witch's evil enchantment."

Liberals who were more interested in electoral victories than in miraculous kisses—George McGovern, for one—put scarcely less stock in the boom generation's potential power. Fred Dutton, a McGovern adviser in 1972, cast a yearning eye on the eighteen-to-twenty-one-year-old voters who had been enfranchised the year before. "The politics of the '70s offers one of those rare chances to rally a new following, or at least to provoke a new configuration, out of this immense sector of younger voters. . . . If an exciting individual or cause really stirs this generation, it could be activated in numbers that make irrelevant any past indicator of political participation among the young, and it would then become one of the few human waves of historic consequence." When liberalism, or at least McGovern's brand of it, produced no human waves, the effort was carried on into the '80s by neoliberals. (No one seems to like the word, but that's all right, no one seems to like the politicians, either.) McGovern's campaign manager, Gary Hart, wrote in his post-1972 book, *Right from the Start*, of "the ineluctable tide of new generations," a tide he professed to be able to harness for his own Presidential runs.

It isn't just liberals who have an interest in the subject. Libertarians, much taken with analyses which break the electorate down, not in halves, left and right, but in quarters—liberal, conservative, populist, and libertarian—identify the fourth quarter—themselves—with the aging boom generation, which they see as the key to political success. "Entrepreneurs," says David Boaz, vice-president of the Cato Institute, a libertarian think tank in Washington, D.C., "have arisen to satisfy every other desire of the baby boom from hula hoops to Saabs. . . . The politician who sees the yuppie market and capitalizes on it" is headed for victory.

There was a moment, finally, about the time Ronald Reagan was being hallooed at Ohio State, when Republicans thought the generations were breaking for them. There had been hopeful talk in the late '60s from the direction of the Ripon Society of a new coalition consisting of liberal Republicans, blacks, and young people: Lindsayism. By the mid-'80s, the heirs of the young and formerly young seemed to be the Republican right. *Sub regno Reagan*, the young voters of the post-boom were registering Republican in unprecedented numbers, and the boom generation itself seemed to be tilting toward the GOP. The El Dorado of realignment, which has shimmered in Republican brains since it was first glimpsed by Kevin Phillips in 1968, looked to be taking on solidity, with boom and post-boom support. Among the hopeful steps George Bush took to secure these new Republicans was to pick the first member of the boom generation to run on a national ticket—Dan Quayle.

What came of all these hopes was nothing. If the handicappers of the younger generations had worked on Wall Street, they would have been reduced to peddling umbrellas and fell-off-the-back-of-truck books from tables in front of Trinity Church. Corporations outlasted bell-bottoms. George McGovern carried fewer states than Winfield Scott. "I think we exaggerated the amount of enthusiasm for change among young people," he told Hunter Thompson sourly post-debacle. "There really are a great number of people in this country that are a helluva lot more interested in whether the Dolphins beat the Redskins." The only baby boomer Gary Hart reached out and touched was Donna Rice. As an exercise in political entrepreneurship, libertarianism resembles a sun-activated drape opener more than a Saab. John Lindsay became a Democrat, then history. So far from being a pied piper for his peers, young Senator Quayle had more than he could do to hold off old Senator Bentsen, and Republican realignment turned out to be just another mirage, the Senate, which the GOP had held for six years, having slipped back into Democratic hands, and the House looking gerrymandered until the next century.

What happened? Since these various hopes were mutually exclusive, they could not all have been fulfilled. But the success of none of them suggests a more general problem. Maybe no one found a way to use the boom generation or its successors for political purposes because those generations didn't exist in the first place. Instead of spending their time looking for explanations for the behavior of twenty- and thirty- and forty-year-olds, the experts would have done better to acknowledge the fact that there are no generations, in a politically coherent sense, at all.

The very first failure of a boom hypothesis (a sober boom hypothesis, not Reich's visions) should have made the point. In July of 1972 the Gallup poll showed college students preferring McGovern to Nixon 61% to 35%. This certainly looked like Dutton's human wave. By October, the gap had closed to 49–47. At his victory celebration a month later, Nixon boasted that he had won a majority of the youth vote, something that had been "thought to be impossible." Believers in left-of-center versions of the boom hypothesis could save the hypothesis only by falling back on personalities: George McGovern was a bad campaigner, hobbled by worse running mates. Indeed, they continue to reach for personality every time the hypothesis is in trouble: Michael Dukakis had no charm, Gary Hart had too much, Joe Biden/Dick Gephardt/(fill in the blank) were (fill in the blank). There is a simpler answer: that the boom generation, like every other, is politically heterogeneous. Ohio State did not suddenly come into existence in 1984. There were always Ohio States.

The universe of politics is big. It is true that eligibility requirements cut down the number of American adults who can vote, and that the percentage of eligible voters who do vote is one of the lowest in any democracy. Still, politics is one of the largest catchments in American life. If a hundred thousand people buy a hardcover book, it makes *The New York Times* best-seller list. Five hundred thousand sales is a blockbuster. The Judith Krantzes of the world can make the low millions. Eighty-eight million people voted in the last Presidential election. Any variety American life has will show up here. It would be astonishing if anything as broadly defined as an age group showed predictable, much less revolutionary, behavior in such a setting.

This common-sense conclusion bucks the perception that,

for a while—people get hazy about just when the while was, but let's say 1968—the entire boom generation was mysteriously on one psychic wavelength, which imprinted it (*must have* imprinted it) ever after. But that perception is an artifact of culture, and of publicity. Two years ago, one of the news weeklies commemorated the twentieth anniversary of the *annus mirabilis* by running a series of then-and-now shots—the then pictures in black-and-white, as if color film hadn't been invented yet—of countercultural icons: Black Panthers, the Grateful Dead, Timothy Leary. This, the contrast was meant to say, was the way we were. There was only one thing missing: little black-and-white reproductions of covers and photo spreads from *Time*, *Newsweek*, *Life*, and *Look* of the twenty years earlier. Those stories (all assembled, incidentally, by members of the pre-boom generation) did not by any means always approve of what was going on among young people. But they contributed powerfully to the nation's sense that this—the seeding, if not the greening, of America—was what *was* going on. The young people who supplied the footage, or who learned from the finished products, so far from being rebels, were teachers' pets.

The one issue on which the boom generation can be said to have exerted some special influence, unexplainable by normal political heterogeneity, was the Vietnam War. Even here, the antiwar push from the young was not due so much to numbers —there were pro-war and indifferent people in the age group all along—as to intensity. This sentiment had less to do with any peculiar generational traits—narcissism, independent-mindedness, whatever—as with the quite simple fact that it was young men who stood to be drafted, for no very clear reason. The second factor is as important as the first. Americans will fight wars; they will even submit to conscription. But without a sinking of the *Lusitania* or an attack on Pearl Harbor, they are traditionally reluctant. The Johnson administration supplied no compelling rationale for overcoming that reluctance. Nixon was both more forthright and forthrightly engaged in a strategic retreat.

What other issues in which the boom is supposed to be particularly concerned can honestly be laid to its door? Sex, and its political fallout? Yes, the boom generation got a lot of it, or at least talked about it. But they were scarcely alone. A lot of people had tickets on the sexual express. The couples in *Couples* did not belong to the baby boom. Neither did John Updike, their creator. Ditto Alexander Portnoy and Philip Roth. We saw a lot of young bodies during the sexual revolution, because they're prettier to look at. But older limbs got a workout, too. Philip Larkin thought sexual intercourse, which "began in 1963," was "rather late for me." He was forty-one at the time. He was wrong.

What about the tax revolt—the next boom project, after settling down into *Big Chill* wage earning and monogamy? Once again, the aging youngsters who went along with it were part of a larger swell. Ronald Reagan, who cut the top income-tax rate, was old enough to be a boom grandfather, and Howard Jarvis, who wrote Proposition 13, was old enough to be Reagan's uncle. Their success had a lot more to do with the conjunction of rising tax rates and a stagflating economy, and the pain that that caused everyone, than with the predilections of a single generation.

The disposition to look for generational explanations represents the last stage of materialism, which is mysticism. The political materialist is always on the lookout for some condition—class and ethnic group are two of the more popular—from which to deduce the behavior of masses of people. Since money and culture are powerful factors, the materialist is often perceptive in a rough-and-ready way, though he always risks being blind-sided when new states of mind appear which cut across his categories. The mystic, seeking to imitate the materialist, imputes a factitious reality to some impressive-looking but, in fact, trivial trait —a common birthdate, for instance—to which he assigns, with even less justification, the same predictive power. Materialists at least talk about something, though it is not always relevant. Mystics talk about nothing. In the case of the baby boom and its relation to politics, there is also a personal motivation that has to do with fees and prestige. Just as it is in the interests of the Catholic pollster Andrew Greeley to find continuing differences between Protestant and Catholic behavior—otherwise what need would there be for priestly pollsters?—so it is in the interests of graying flacks to claim that they have a congenital insight into a politically important matter—otherwise they might not be paid so much to run or comment on the next campaign.

The real force for change in politics turns out to be what it always was: ideas. These are less common than one might think in a culture as wordy as ours has become. But when an idea exists, and has a wide influence, the effects are long-lasting. America, for example, maintains garrisons in South Korea and West Germany, and treaty structures that justify the garrisons, because of ideas about American security which first appeared in places like the Long Telegram and the "Mr. X" article, then impressed a portion of the political elite, and finally persuaded a majority of the people at large. The garrisons remain, despite a certain puzzled dissatisfaction with their being there, and a lack of any sense of urgency about their present mission, because no superseding idea has emerged to justify their removal—though as these words are written, Gorbachev labors to supply one.

Ideas do not have to persuade all the eighty-eight million. (Short of mother love, what could?) They don't have to, to be politically successful. The rock-bottom base of any nominee of a major party in the modern era, Goldwaters and McGoverns included, is about 40%. In a less lopsided contest, a politician who can give 5% of the voters some reason to cross over and vote for him is headed for the White House. The politician who can persuade 10% is headed for a landslide.

It is true that Gary Hart, one of the leading apostles of generational mysticism, also talked about the importance of new ideas. But the ideas he actually offered—military reform, industrial policy—were too small-bore to sustain the kind of political upheaval he sought. The most important new idea in his arsenal turned out to be the need for a new generation of leaders (that ineluctable tide again) led by himself. If he had actually had a new idea, he might be halfway through his second term now. Lacking any, he is where he is. Nothing fails like inevitability.

Here is my notion of a possibly successful political idea, which we have already seen in the Gephardt and Jackson campaigns two years ago—and in the campaigns of Walter Mondale and John Connally before that—and which we may see again in 1992. That is protection. Protectionists never call themselves that, of course, and if they succeed, they will have earned the victor's right to call themselves anything they like. But let's call them protectionists for now.

Protection is unique in being an idea that has been disdained by illuminati of the right and left alike. Postwar conservative intellectuals opposed it on free-market grounds; liberals of *The New York Times* variety resisted it as a threat to internationalism. Lately, however, that unanimity has been crumbling. It will not crumble all the way, and it need not. All an idea needs is enough credentialed thinkers backing it to save it from the stigma of yahoodom.

There is also a potential audience. Looking at the ten states that Michael Dukakis carried, we see that some of them—Rhode Island, West Virginia, Hawaii—are simple bastions, which will vote for any Democrat who is photosensitive. The rest were mostly states historically interested in environmentalism and "good government"—call them goo-goo states—stretching across the north of the country in a band: Washington, Oregon, Minnesota, Wisconsin; Dukakis also lost Vermont by only 51–49. This is the Democratic base in a Presidential election. But he also carried agriculturally depressed Iowa, and missed carrying farm- and rust-belt Illinois and rust-belt Pennsylvania by Vermont-sized margins. Here is a potential target of opportunity. A Democrat who could add to the goo-goo states most of everything between Denver and Pittsburgh would be in striking distance of winning. California would put him over the top. The protectionist pitch depends on the economy heading south, but of course if it doesn't head south, the next Democratic Presidential candidate might as well stay home. If the economy does sag, however, some Democrat could approach the hardest-hit heartland with the argument that the crafty Japanese did it all, buying our farmland and dumping their cheap little cars, and the about-to-be united Europeans, led by the Germans, will do worse. America fought these countries fifty years ago. Why can't it fight for itself now?

This is not a good idea. Indeed, I believe it is wrong and, in its grosser forms, evil. But it is the kind of idea that could appeal to strategically placed people who are fifty-five as well as those who are twenty-five, those who remember Frank Sinatra as well as those who remember Bruce Springsteen. As such, it is the kind of idea that makes the tectonic plates of politics shift.

It's a long way from paint-throwing Yalies. But then, most of us were never there in the first place.

The Split-Level Generation

Walter Olson

A few years back, rumors began to circulate that the generation of the '60s and '70s, having moved on from the leftishness of its youth, was now showing symptoms of leaning toward libertarianism, the viewpoint said (with cartoonish simplification) to meld the conservative's support for economic freedom with the liberal's support for civil liberties. Upon first hearing these reports, I admit to having raised a dubious eyebrow, for I spent my campus years in the early '70s hawking this particular line of politico-economic wares with sad unsuccess.

The conservative half of the message was perhaps a lost cause from the start. The major split among those few classmates of mine with vocal opinions on political economy was, for all I could tell, between those who favored nationalizing everything down to people's combs and toothbrushes and those who thought taking just the "commanding heights" of the economy might be enough. The other division was between the wistful ones who hoped that post-revolutionary industry could be managed by workers' or consumers' co-ops (which dimly seemed like much the same thing) and those with a better sense of the historical dynamics of revolutionary power. In such an atmosphere, my urgings that they look into the arguments for the privatization of lighthouses must have seemed not so much reactionary as positively Martian.

Much more unexpected, and consequently harder to take, was the lack of interest in the *laissez-faire* agenda on social issues. Full-brew libertarianism yields no jot or tittle in its championing of individual rights, and thus rejects out of hand such infringements of personal liberty as, for openers, the military draft, censorship, and drug laws. This, I thought, would at least provide a few points of agreement and repose amid the inevitable late-night debates. No such luck. On the drug issue, to begin with, the campus was an effective free zone against arrest, and that was apparently all that even steady users asked for. The draft was more of a looming threat, but hardly ever did I hear it denounced in principle. The cutting-edge progressive opinion seemed to be that conscription might not be so bad were U.S. troops only being sent to help, rather than hinder, the armed insurgencies in question. Anyway, the alternative, a better-paid volunteer army, was all too likely to fill up with ambitious youths from poorer backgrounds, which somehow seemed unfair compared with keeping military pay low and filling the jobs by coercive lottery. (Yes, the logic is shaky, but it was good enough for Ted Kennedy.)

Free speech? That definitely aroused strong passions—but from the wrong direction. The perennial controversy was over whether this or that crank racialist or retired army general, or even the state's Republican governor, should be allowed to speak on campus at all. Those who favored shouting down or otherwise driving away such unwelcome visitors may not have been a majority, but they won most of the practical battles.

The spirit of censorship was just then beginning to get a grip (since then much consolidated) on the American academy. Third World protesters had occupied the offices of our venerable college daily and made it agree to install a "community" functionary to vet each edition the night before for material deemed too hot to publish. (After the demonstrators had left, the editors wriggled out of their promise.) Still fresh in memory were the disruptions at Cornell and elsewhere that forced a number of eminent conservative scholars from their chairs, an assault on free thought that didn't seem to trouble much of anybody in retrospect.

In short, by the time I encountered it, a few years after its peak, the student movement had pretty much pegged the toleration of opposing views as a bourgeois value—as indeed it is—and had rejected *laissez-faire* in ideas no less than in economics. One slogan on a leaflet of this period sticks in the mind because of its candor: "Free all *progressive* political prisoners in Ethiopia." My emphasis, but their selectivity.

Of course, times changed. In the wider world, the left was beginning to go into decline, and even in the academy, its adherents, once so keen on relevance, were starting to withdraw behind a moated scholasticism of many-footnoted obfuscation. More to the point, there was little reason to extrapolate the attitudes we all struck in campus arguments to the positions we would take later, on the outside, where the pressure to conform would (it turned out) prove to be so much less strong.

So I shouldn't have been all that surprised in later years when I began to run into old debate partners who had shed their radicalism in whole or part. Even the fellow who told me that he would take great pleasure in putting a bullet through my head after the revolution turned out, on second encounter, to have mellowed quite pleasantly. Others who had uttered not a peep of dissent at our Keynes-and-points-left economics lectures turned out to have been inward dissenters all the while, unrecognizable at the time, reading Friedrich Hayek and Milton Friedman by flashlight under their bedcovers.

But however the winds might freshen, caution and temperament still kept me from feeling any soaring political optimism. So many partisans, hopefully eying the demographics, had claimed this generation for their own, and had all been left looking rather foolish when the Age of Aquarius passed and the world moved on to the chill and scaly Age of Pisces. Charles Reich, for one, was quite sure of the Consciousness III victory to come; to "those who have glimpsed the real possibilities of life," he averred, "the prospect of a dreary corporate job, a ranch-house life, or a miserable death in war is utterly intolerable."

The revolutionary aspirations, as so often happens, enjoyed not a complete romantic failure but a far more mortifying partial success. Since *The Greening of America* began to oxidize at the edges, progress has been made on all three of the complained-of utter intolerabilities. Developers have started building more houses with staircases for buyers who dislike the ranch layout; personnel managers at the better companies now work hard to make corporate jobs more varied and stimulating; foreign-policy officials have looked after U.S. interests abroad while arranging (at this writing at least) for an entire generation of Americans to avoid death in war, miserable or otherwise. Almost anyone who does not care for suburbia can choose to live in a gritty city neighborhood, at some risk of contributing to the de-funkification thereof.

The higher the peak of presumption, the bumpier the road down; as someone has said, nothing dates like a wave of the future. Summer of Love memorabilia, now turning up in collectibles shops alongside atomic-age ashtrays and World of Tomorrow knickknacks, like those draw their power as *kitsch* from the palpable nature of the failed aspiration. It may take a while, however, for the pop artifacts produced between 1966 and 1972 really to catch on as period furnishings; to me at least they seem more foreign, more profoundly estranged from the current scene, than anything from the '50s. Those of us who arrived at college a year or two after the peace movement peaked were already becoming cynics on the subject of student idealism. I recall an older classmate's remark that the squat sugar bowls of hotel china in our dining halls dated back only a few years. "There were silver bowls until the '60s," he explained, "but they were all ripped off by the Most Idealistic Generation in History."

. . .

If there is one sane thing about libertarians (and I'm sure there is more than one), it is that most of us feel no urge to pose as the wave of the future. Back when our basic views traveled under the heading of classical liberalism, after all, they were for a very long time the settled convictions of most enlightened people around the world. Then, at some point—World War I has been cited as the pivotal event, though some observers would go forward to 1933 and others back to 1848—the idea of individual liberty was cast aside almost everywhere in favor of the modern pack of state-centered ideologies: nationalism, socialism, corporatism, and all the rest. The habit of mind of surviving classical liberals was one of bunkered embattlement; had our views begun to revive, we would have been the last to notice.

Then, suddenly, just such a revival, in America as well as Eastern Europe, was being trumpeted on the front pages. Even my friend Dave Boaz of the Cato Institute, who is nearly as gloomy as I on most of these matters, said he thought there was something to these reports of a genuine shift in public opinion, a shift that was in some way connected with the baby boomers. My curiosity aroused, I decided that what was needed was a visit to that wax museum of modern manners and funhouse mirror of national character, the public-opinion poll. I decided to leaf through six years' worth of the magazine *Public Opinion*, whose estimable editor, Karlyn Keene, also sent me two other polls on generational opinion, one by the Yankelovich people and the other by Peter Hart for *Rolling Stone*.

Here are a few advance caveats. Obviously *Public Opinion* did not report all the polls that might have shed light on this subject, and those it did report could be maddeningly variable. (In 1984, of voters who considered themselves liberals, how many went for Reagan? Twenty-five percent, if you believe ABC's exit polls; 35%, if you credit NBC's. Same day, same election.) As usual in this field, slight rewordings of a question, or a lapse of a few months between poll dates, could produce wide swings in reported opinion. Accordingly, I concentrated on assessing differences between age groups *within* a given poll, and was inclined, unless a sample size was very large, to disregard variations of less than ten points or so.

The surprises were several—and, on the whole, pleasant.

Voting preferences may not always have much to do with political philosophy, but they are the subject of the most copious and reliable polling data, so I started there. As a predictor of balloting patterns, however, age, or more precisely generational affiliation, is much overrated. Young people lurch around a bit in their voting choices, but by thirty or so this fickleness seems to subside, and they mostly vote much as their parents and grandparents do in the same elections.

Consider the cohort of Americans who reached their twenty-first birthdays between 1957 and 1971—the JFK-to-Woodstock generation, if you will. They include the first major wave of the baby boom, along with some from the baby trough that came before. In 1972, a group heavily overlapping this one was the backbone of George McGovern's Presidential candidacy, giving him support ten points or more higher than the average voter. Eight years later, by the time Reagan ran against Carter, all traces of this youthful frolic had been washed from the sand. The group gave Reagan precisely the same 56% of their vote as did older groups. The vast literature on the "generation gap" was ready to be pulped and sent to the landfills, at least as far as Reaganite proclivities were any indication.

Since then, although results differ from poll to poll, not much lasting or consistent evidence has shown that baby boomers vote much differently from their elders. No significant age differences emerged in the 1984 Presidential or House races, for example. Such small generational differences in party affiliation as can be observed have a look about them of the transient or accidental. The oldest group of voters, those now at retirement age, disproportionately identify themselves as Democrats, but tend not to carry this preference over to corresponding views on public issues. The youngest, those born after 1960, were at first the least inclined to vote for Reagan, but then, within a few years, veered to become a shade more Republican than the rest.

The canyons that yawn wide in American elections are not so much between generations as between such groups as home-owners and renters, say, or married and single people. The married/single polarity in particular seems to be to this era of voting patterns what Civil War sympathies were to those of a century ago. In one poll, matrimony explained a staggering twenty-three to twenty-six points of difference between the major parties, while the supposedly seminal distinction between blue-collar and executive/professional jobholders explained only five to ten points. (My free advice to the Republicans: Forget about collar colors and age waves and launch a crash program to marry off the U.S. population, preferably ensuring each pair of newlyweds a house with a mortgage.)

As hinted earlier, party affiliation is at best a low-grade sort of evidence on whether people hold any particular views on the rightful purpose of government. We of the libertarian ilk are split many ways and form no firm voting bloc. Most often we are identified as a Republican constituency, providing a counter-weight within GOP counsels to the influence of fundamentalists and other social conservatives. But many of us are found among independents and disgusted nonvoters; some root for the tiny Libertarian party, while a surprising number go Democratic, attracted by that party's perceived social liberalism, or sometimes by its less assertive approach to foreign policy, though privately regretting its domestic identification with government-as-smotherer.

The age patterns on liberal versus conservative identification can likewise be at best suggestive. Those of classical-liberal or libertarian views are typically lumped in these days with the right (much to the annoyance of Friedrich Hayek, who went to the trouble of writing an essay entitled "Why I Am Not a Conservative"). For what it is worth, those in the thirtyish age bracket are less likely than others to consider "liberal" a pejorative word, but not much more likely to adopt the word to describe themselves.

We reach firmer ground with polls on more specific controversies. Here, too, however, very many questions bring out no discernible difference between the older groups and the baby boomers. On economics, for example, those in their thirties and early forties have clearly turned marketward in their views—but, then, so has nearly everyone else this side of Ralph Nader and the *Village Voice*. There may be a story here about the renewal of free-market views, but it is not specifically a story of the baby boomers; though there may have been a great revolution in public opinion, it has not been a great replacement of one generation's opinions by another's. The same appears to hold true on a wide range of other issues, from military spending to the use of force against terrorism to the erstwhile nuclear freeze to affirmative action: allowing for the variability of poll data, few real differences between generations are apparent.

The issues where age groups unmistakably diverge form a contiguous if sprawling territory to which it is hard to assign a name any more exact than "social issues." They include free speech; many (but not all) issues of race; sexual morality and the role of women; and civil liberties, broadly defined. Some of the differences on matters racial are quite dramatic. Wide gaps, for example, appear on what you might call social-acceptance indicators, such as willingness to vote for a candidate of another race with congenial political views. By a massive thirty-five-point margin, boomers are more likely to oppose laws against interracial marriage. (Hard as it may be to imagine today, many states kept such laws on their books right down to the '60s, when the Supreme Court declared them invalid.)

One should always avoid the facile analogy between race and gender, but almost as large a generational skew showed up in views of sex and sex roles. Younger respondents were much more likely to approve of having mothers join the work force. By thirty-one points, another huge chasm in the polling landscape, the younger groups were less likely to see cohabitation outside marriage as always wrong. By a twenty-one-point margin, the boomers were more tolerant of gays (with a slight falling off among the next-younger respondents). Support for abortion on demand, though not a very reliable litmus test for libertarian sentiment—too many sincere people have applied the principle of noncoercion and come out on the anti-abortion side—was, I note for the record, stronger by sixteen points among the boomers.

The biggest difference on any single major issue, forty points, was on whether pornography for adult use should be banned. This may or may not have anything to do with a changing view of the sexes. Quite possibly it derives instead from a more general disapproval of censorship, because those under forty were strenuously opposed to curbs on political opinion. In particular, they were vastly less eager than older respondents to prevent holders of unpopular opinions from lecturing in public or teaching in universities, or to stop public libraries from stocking books by such authors. The gaps here were always of at least twenty points, usually thirty and often forty.

This streak of anti-authoritarian sentiment seems to carry over to a number of other issues that could be grouped under an awning of civil liberties. Boomers were far less willing to condone letting the government tap phones or forcing people to testify against themselves in times of national emergency. By thirty points plus, they were less likely to endorse the notion that "any person who hides behind the law when he is questioned about his activities doesn't deserve much consideration."

An interesting pattern seemed to emerge when the wording of a question varied from poll to poll (though such differences should always be interpreted with caution). When a matter of race or gender roles was phrased with reference to toleration or the widening of opportunities or the wrongness of treating individuals invidiously, it did much better among our group than among the older respondents. When it was phrased to suggest a more active and ongoing government role, the generational differences tended to melt away. Not to say, again, that government programs were uniformly unpopular. As usual, that depended on how a question was phrased. It's only that programs with a statist flavor did not pick up a big *generational* boost. Almost any civil-rights proposal couched as a way to combat discrimination, for example, creates a generational split; but when asked whether minorities should get explicit preferences, boomers like the idea no better than anyone else.

An arguably similar effect shows up in questions about laws requiring companies to grant "parental leave" (i.e., force them to hold open the jobs of workers who take time off to care for a baby). Most of those surveyed seem to view this as a straight role-of-women issue: Are you in favor of mothers who want to go back to jobs while their kids are still tiny, or agin 'em? As such, the results break down almost entirely on generational lines, as opposed to lines of, say, income or profession. But when one survey worded the question so as to call attention to the coercive nature of the proposal as a regulation of business, opinion shifted in a notable way. This poll included along with its pro and con sides a third position: that it would be nice if employers offered this kind of leave, but they should not be forced to do so. This "nice, but not required" position was apt to appeal to the modern libertarian; it signals moral support for the working mother without trying to force the market for workplace benefits to develop faster than it naturally would. The thirty-to-forty-fours were still, on balance, for the coercive law, but by a much reduced margin, and the "nice, but not required" position did better among them than among any other group. I think libertarians can take guarded solace.

Likewise, the boomers were somewhat more impatient than their elders with class distinctions as a social barrier—but no more inclined than anyone else to endorse the proposition that "government should do something to reduce income differentials between rich and poor." This is entirely consistent with the classical-liberal view, which celebrates social mobility but recognizes that government redistribution of wealth tends to hamper that process.

It is important not to overstate the case. The boomers come out less libertarian than their elders on a number of issues. They are more likely, for example, to support "fair housing" laws and school busing, although both measures come at a price in individual autonomy. The scattered opinion trends, then, do not add up to the sort of consistent commitment to individual rights that libertarians might wish. But they do suggest that the pundits' general formulation of the boomers' views—social but not economic liberalism—is not too far off base.

What is intriguing is how bitterly this combination of views is reproached, and from how very many directions. Leftist commentators appear more upset by the generation's evident lack of a Robin Hood sensibility than they are consoled by its enlightened attitudes on social issues. Plenty of rightists, meanwhile, suspect that the boomers are still soft on acid, amnesty, and abortion, and take no comfort at their apparently tranquil acceptance of America and its way of life. Leaders of organized labor and organized religion, who have seen their flocks stray and scatter in these later years, perennially berate the thirtyish for their lack of a properly functioning conscience. (Criticism began with, but could not be limited to, the "yuppies"; as usual, the most affluent are too few in number to be driving wider opinion trends.)

The besetting sins of the baby boomers are widely agreed to be selfishness and hedonism. Spiritually, the boomers are accused of leading atomistic existences, bereft of both social involvement and meaningful inner lives, if they ever had them; politically, they are said to be hypocrites, claiming to believe in progress but unwilling to do anything about it by shelling out of their own pockets. To top it off, they want to legalize all their own vices. The idiotically extravagant praise of the '60s has been turned on its head: we are dealing here with the most depraved generation in memory, if not in history.

Much of this blame-mongering, it seems to me, simply springs from the nearly universal tendency to ascribe political differences to character flaws. Baby boomers show no enthusiasm for being heavily taxed and regulated, so they must be cold and selfish. One problem (you would think) with this argument is that older groups are nowadays no more enthusiastic about being taxed and regulated, but it is an easy jump to the idea that the coldness and selfishness in question are not specifically generational but afflict the American population as a reprehensible whole.

It would be just as easy (if, to opponents, less satisfying) to ascribe the boomers' apparent views to practical experience. They are reaching middle age in an era where free markets and low taxes have plainly clobbered government direction and high taxes on every dimension of productivity; where contraception has worked a revolution in sexual mores; and where advances in communication technology are starting to make old-fashioned censorship virtually ineffective unless it is tyrannical. As for why the older generation (formerly) held less libertarian opinions, it is equally unnecessary to finger such character defects as, say, envy and meddlesomeness; one might instead point to their experience with a Depression that brought business competition into disrepute, a world war that called for decisive central government, and so forth.

The polls do not in any case lend much support to the prevalent complaints about hypocrisy. Among the relatively few instances I could find of a sizable generation gap on an economic question was on whether Social Security benefits needed to be raised. The difference between the baby boomers and the elderly was a substantial twenty points. Many will routinely assume that both sides were trying to get theirs. Not so. The differences cut *against* the grain of self-interest. Only 43% of the elderly themselves favored the raise, but 63% of the boomers said they thought it was desirable. Or again: another pollster asked whether discrimination against elderly people was a big problem in America. Only 15% of the elderly themselves said it was, but twice as many of the baby boomers, around 30%, thought the problem was serious. Results like these are not easy to explain on a theory that myopic self-interest drives political opinion. "Public choice" scholars, call your office.

If this generation faces a test of hypocrisy, it comes on the free speech issue, because control of expression is so often speciously reconciled with idealism. There was reason to be pessimistic here, given what has happened on American campuses, where what started as the shouting down of isolated speakers has developed into a fairly elaborate scheme of repression of thought and speech. One college after another has revamped its disciplinary code to come down hard on the disk jockey who allows call-in listeners to crack ethnic jokes, the literature professor who expounds Eurocentric views in class, the wayward fraternity brother who whistles at the wrong passer-by. State and private campuses alike have moved to suppress satirical leaflets and posters, impudent questions by students in class, and similar conduct that runs afoul of the ubiquitous Joke Police and Wink Patrol. (Q. How many feminists does it take to change a light bulb? A. *That's not funny.*)

Outside the academy as well as in, the great majority of boomers have little use for racial slurs or the more invidious forms of flirtation; but, to judge by the polls, they also make a big deal of free expression. This is their acid test on hypocrisy. They pass. Not only do the polls find them willing to let racists and other detested groups write, speak, and organize freely; by very wide margins they are *more* willing to tolerate such speech than are the (less racially sensitized) older respondents. The current outbreak of sensitivity fascism (as it has irreverently been called) should not be taken as representative of the generation that came of age in the '60s and '70s; from all evidence, that generation is determined to tolerate the views it loathes, not just the views it finds congenial.

But back to the charges of spiritual emptiness. The polls, versatile as they are, can shed an oblique sort of light even here. Surveys have periodically asked people how happy or contented they are—admittedly a vague question—and the responses I have seen show a strange evenness. For each age group, the answers come out the same: one third of us are extremely happy, one sixth are quite miserable, and the other 50% find themselves in between. (Do the same people go on being happy through life, I wonder, or is there rotation? I couldn't find out.)

The boomers, then, are as happy by self-report as their parents. Perhaps they are besotted by material opulence, which consoles them for their failure to find human-scale joys? Not very likely: it was the older groups that, as one might expect, were much more likely to report being happy with their financial situation. Some less tangible source of contentment must be warming hearts. One clue may be found in a 1986 Yankelovich poll of people in their thirties (this one did not give age-group comparisons, so it should be taken more cautiously). By wide margins, the respondents said that the single most fully satisfactory aspect of their existence, and also the single aspect that had most turned out better than they expected at age twenty-one, was their family life.

I do tire of hearing the baby boomers attacked as selfish and hedonistic as they reach the very point in their lives when they become most productive, supporting their families and the rest of society with most devotion and least complaint. For much the same reasons, I tire of hearing the same attacks wheeled out against libertarian views and policies. To let people keep the proceeds of their work and savings is to encourage productiveness, not dissipation. To forswear imposing one's values on one's neighbors is to be a model of self-restraint, not self-aggrandizement. Real grabbiness, real look-out-for-number-oneism, comes to full weedy flower when people start using the government to run each other's lives and live at each other's expense—the sort of thing that peaked in the interest-group politics of the late '70s.

Conceivably, self-interest might underlie some of the boomers' views on social issues. No doubt people in their thirties are more likely than people in their seventies to smoke marijuana, have abortions, or cohabit with an unmarried partner. Or, more to the point these days, more of them probably retain incense-scented memories of doing such things, or have younger friends whom they would not like to see getting a police record for the same conduct. As these memories and friendships fade, perhaps the principles will fade, too, and the jailing of draft resisters and busting of head shops no longer will seem like such an atrocity; they may even learn to accept and embrace what in such freighted terminology are called the policies of "zero tolerance."

I take a more optimistic view. Manners and mores have indeed tightened up beyond all expectations, in what Ellen Willis has called the long slide from *Yes I said yes I will yes* to *Just say No.* It would be one thing if the boomers had given up their wild ways because they were converted to a different metaphysics. But the truth is simply that they found that wild ways don't work. Most stopped using drugs because direct experience, or at least close observation, teaches that after a while it becomes boring and wasteful, health problems aside. Most stopped sleeping around because empirically it tends to make all sides miserable, health problems once again aside.

Conservative mores founded on experience have some advantages over conservative mores founded on superstition or presupposition. They may call for temperance or for abstinence, depending on the context, but in either case they proceed from an ideal of self-control and chosen loyalty, not obedience to authority; of understanding and mastering danger, not running from it in panic. This knowing kind of conservatism is perfectly consistent with accepting the married, sober, and socially woven-in as the norm, but recognizes, too, the folly of subjecting the fringe to furious repression. Whatever the rest of our legacy, I think those of us who grew up in the '60s and '70s are headed for this sort of split-level compromise: private lives too domestic and restrained to satisfy the avant-garde, but public views too tolerant and expansive to please the reactionaries. And I think we'll get it just about right.

Break Glass in Case of Emergency

George Sim Johnston

Although I now blush to acknowledge it, one afternoon when I was a junior in college I placed a pomegranate before the picture of a well-known Eastern mystic. This happened in a Transcendental Meditation Center which had set up shop near campus. Once the fruit was in place, my "instructor" turned to me and began to intone my mantra. I promised never to reveal it, but you can hear it in a dozen movies set in the mysterious East—it's that prolonged aching vowel, presumably some fakir at his prayers, which throbs on the sound track while the camera pans the spires of Baghdad. I politely repeated it, and when my instructor (whom I saw a week later taking the Law Boards) was satisfied, he led me to a bare room and left me alone so that I could go on repeating it. The mantra did not improve on acquaintance. That weird Asiatic murmur was as soothing as fingernails on the blackboard. I gave up the whole business before summer vacation. But like certain tunes that won't go away, the mantra strays into my mind now and then, a final retreating echo of the odd campus culture of the early '70s.

I suppose what I was seeking on that spring afternoon was what one Freudian writer has called a "manipulable sense of well-being." The point of the mantra, apart from putting me in touch with the infinite Ground of Being, was to make me feel well-adjusted, healthy, at ease with things. This was a major under-graduate preoccupation at the time. All were busy getting their heads together. The phrase sounds antique now, but you always heard it from classmates who were dropping out for a semester. They would pack a copy of *The Prophet* and a few James Taylor albums and head for Cape Cod or some other vale of Kashmir. Generally they came back more crazed than ever. But the quest never abated. The goal was an interior peace that could be ma-nipulated like the graphic equalizer on a sound system. This, I submit, is the great and seldom-achieved prize of modern secular culture, and it is not surprising that the search for it is often conducted through a maze of religiosity.

Once out of college, we had a great deal of money thrown at us, but the prosperity did not make anyone abandon the search. Indeed, the material abundance created an uneasiness which is not to be found in societies reared on scarcity. The wraith and ghost of it were reported in magazine articles with titles like "Baby Boom Blues." But it would be a mistake to reduce our vague complaints to sociology. Yes, we are subject to pains that would be difficult to explain to a Masai herdsman; but we are also heir to an interior restlessness which St. Augustine diagnosed sixteen hundred years ago: "We were made for thee, O God, and our hearts are restless until they rest in thee." Whether he likes it or not, man is driven to transcend himself. What the money did for baby boomers was to multiply the pos-sible substitutes for the Almighty.

The competition between God and Mammon is probably no more heated today than it was in the past. The American formula has always been, in Henry James's words, "to make so much money that you won't, that you don't 'mind,' don't mind anything. . . ." A young MBA once put this in the vernacular when he told me that his goal was to make ten million dollars of "fuck-you" money. As far as I know, he hasn't made it; but it is noticeable that those baby boomers who make enough money to live out the Jamesian formula (they tend to be on Wall Street) have mid-life crises earlier than most. As for the rest, the trance of merchandise is broken now and then, and they look around for something to believe in. For my generation, this urge toward transcendence has generally fastened onto four activities: sex, politics, health, and finally—when nothing else seemed to work —religious faith itself.

Sex, as Malcolm Muggeridge has said, is the mysticism of a materialist society. For about twenty years, from the mid-'60s to the mid-'80s, baby boomers enjoyed a window in this particular area that was unprecedented and is not likely to be repeated. Sex had once been the religion of a handful of intellectuals and bohemians; after the pill, the whole middle class got into the act. But the window is closing now, especially for women who have finally figured out that "sexual liberation" is pig heaven for men. The smorgasbord of sexual diseases, moreover, has put recreational sex on a decidedly unspiritual level. I recently heard about a contemporary—a friend of a friend—who spent months trying to seduce a particular woman. After they finally got into his apartment, turned out the lights and disrobed, she announced that she had herpes. They played records instead, and no one called anyone angel of the morning.

The only party still pushing sex as a spiritual anodyne is the New Age movement. Its sexual message derives from Tantric Buddhism, whose obscenities and superstitions spread through northern India in the early Middle Ages. I have before me a catalogue of New Age workshops conducted by a "Holistic Learning Center" in New York. Among the offerings are "Earth-Honoring: The New Male Sexuality" and "Conscious Sexuality." I will spare you the mystical babble of the writeups. The perennial attraction of this brand of mysticism, apart from the not-so-subtle narcissism, is the cosmic license it gives to the unbridled indulgence of the sexual appetites.

But I think most of us, once past the hormonal onslaught of adolescence, would tacitly agree with a remark of the late George Homans, one of the last great Boston Brahmins to get tenure at

Harvard. Professor Homans would pause during his lecture on African kinship patterns, look down on his undergraduate sociology class—a sea of denim and workshirts—and say impressively, "Let's come off it, ladies and gentlemen: sex is not *that* important."

If money and fornication did not quite satisfy the higher impulses of my generation, politics seemed a more sure thing. Political commitment as a substitute for religion is, of course, *the* spiritual syndrome of the twentieth century. "Instead of eternal life," wrote Malraux, "we have the revolution." I matriculated at one of the flash points of the student revolt. Politics was everywhere on campus: shouted from megaphones, handed out in dining halls, sponged up overnight on shop windows; you could not escape it in the darkest depths of the library stacks. Before the end of freshman registration, we quietly put aside the notion of an Ivy League campus as a place where one reclined in the shadows with a volume of Plutarch, and we prepared ourselves for the days of rage.

But the Movement, as it was called, evaporated with astonishing rapidity. In the spring of 1970, after Nixon invaded Cambodia, the administration sent us all home early, free of final exams, so that we could work out our ideals elsewhere. Most of us headed for the beach and returned the next autumn to find that the revolution was over. One reason was that the ideological noise had become irksome. Trotsky's idea of "permanent revolution" means turning up the political Muzak to full volume and keeping it there. Two or three semesters of this were enough. Then there were the militants, whose behavior became a scandal to almost everyone even mildly sympathetic to the New Left agenda. As we watched them spit and hurl obscenities at Irish cops who had families to support or shout down speakers who did not share their exact ideological bias, it seemed as though the characters in Dostoievsky's *The Possessed* had finally opened an American franchise. The whole point of that novel is that radical nihilism is the offspring of a vague progressive liberalism. Were we perhaps getting a glimpse of ourselves a little farther down the road? We drew back with distaste and became yuppies instead.

Marxism itself is merely a secularized version of Christian eschatology, while the more gentle forms of modern progressivism are the debased coin of Christian charity. I believe it was Whittaker Chambers who said that liberalism is charity without the crucifixion. Marxism still has a mystical hold on American academics who have not heard yet that their French friends are on to other things. Since none of Marx's predictions have come true (except the one in *The German Ideology* that socialism imposed on underdeveloped countries would make those countries poorer), it is no longer even pretended that Marxism is a "science." Thus freed from empirical reality, it has become for its disciples an esoteric system of enlightenment (not unlike medieval Kabbala) which need not concern the rest of us—for the time being, anyway.

But everyone else's political indignation slipped out with the ease of a cassette, and their underemployed spiritual impulses had to be parked elsewhere. For some there was a detour into drugs; but the flip side of the same impulse led to the local health club. Health is the last emergent post-Christian religion. Dr. Bernard Nathanson, the former abortionist who is now a leader of the pro-life movement, remarks that modern man seeks "somatic immortality" instead of God. This obsession with Nautilus machines and herbal tea was anticipated by Nietzsche, who predicted that the further man got from the supernatural, the more preoccupied he would be with health. The more Nietzsche himself turned against God, the more obsessed he became with the smallest details of his diet and physical tone. ("No meals between meals," we read in *Ecce Homo*, "no coffee: coffee spreads darkness. . . .")

As a spiritual ruse, exercise and diet will probably have a longer run than sex or politics, if only because they *are* healthy. Or are they, really? Have you ever noticed the people who work in health-food stores? They look like Michael Keaton in *Beetlejuice*. It is always the gaunt spectral souls with circles under their eyes who bring you news of the latest B complex or a zinc pill that lets you get by with less sleep.

There is one other obstacle for baby boomers in their search for God which is so obvious that, like the traffic on Madison Avenue, it is easy to ignore: namely, America itself. The country is blessed with a vernacular culture that makes it the most amusing place to live in the history of the planet. But this funhouse of a republic is the enemy of the interior life. It will not let the mind be still. How do you explain the notion of contemplation, what the ancients meant by "listening to the essence of things," to a trivia-crazed young professional plugged into a Walkman? Interior silence, which every spiritual writer since the Psalms has pointed to as a prerequisite for finding God, is apt to make him so uncomfortable that he will start humming the "Gilligan's Island" theme song.

The lighthearted tone of American life, which is so refreshing in some respects, makes it seem churlish not to shrug off ultimate metaphysical issues. Like death, for example. Whatever happened to death? For medieval man, earthly existence was like the swift passage of a night bird through opposite open windows of a lighted banquet hall; he was acutely aware of the darkness and mystery outside. But the baby boomers, reared in a paradise of distractions, have no trouble keeping such thoughts at bay. It is as though everyone born since 1945 were surrounded by Phil Spector's Wall of Sound (Da Doo Doo Run Run) and protected from any thoughts about what they are doing here and where they are going.

The sheer wonderland that is America—the "crush of strength" and "glittering in the veins" that Wallace Stevens felt on the Connecticut turnpike one night in 1954—is enough to jam the higher frequencies. Such vibrations do not occur among the old stones of Europe. Toward the end of the film *American Graffiti*, a young Richard Dreyfuss stops outside an isolated radio station and looks up at the wires humming in the night and the winking red light of the transmitter that sends the voice of Wolfman Jack to every point of the compass, and he experiences a kind of religious awe. Why go to church when the combination of technology and popular culture can provide such moments?

But a surprising number of baby boomers do go to church —or at least think that it is a good idea. If the available alternatives, from aerobics to Wolfman Jack, can only interpose a temporary ease, all that's left is God. For millennia, religious impulses were taken care of by the Church. But in America, the pluralistic society par excellence, religions tend to behave like amoebas, dividing every five seconds. Talleyrand, complaining about the blandness of the cuisine during his exile, remarked that America has eighty-five religions and only one dish. The ratio has probably not changed for baby boomers, even though they are dining out on octopus tentacles and grilled mesquite free-range chicken.

The bewildering array of spiritualities in this country easily blends into a nice bland pablum that goes down without any problem. Although there are those who try to follow the demanding precepts of traditional religion, most baby boomers find refreshment in a vague religiosity which does not interfere in any way with how they live. In a country where, as Philip Roth put it, "everything goes and nothing matters," and where there is no longer any clericalism in any form except in certain communal isolates like the Hasidim in Brooklyn, you can do whatever you please while keeping an option on eternity. (Break glass in case of emergency.) The religious atmosphere outside the Bible Belt is so soft and yielding that, even if you object to the idea of God, there is no incentive to rebel. The pure atheist in my generation is almost as rare as the pure mystic.

If you are a lapsed Catholic you may, like the hero of *Bright Lights, Big City*, hear on Sunday morning a distant "echo down the marble vaults of your church-going childhood." Or you may actually attend Mass, while inwardly setting aside any church teachings that interfere with self-prescribed notions of well-being. Anna Quindlen, whose recent "Life in the Thirties" column in *The New York Times* could have been subtitled "How to Be an Apostate Catholic and Feel Good About It," is a perfect specimen of baby boom religiosity. Ms. Quindlen asserts that she is a Catholic but goes on to say that she rejects any church teaching that does not suit her—birth control, abortion, Sunday Mass obligation, you name it. "What I do believe in are those guidelines that do not vary from faith to faith," she continues, conveniently forgetting that abortion has been condemned by every major Protestant and Jewish theologian of the twentieth century. But Ms. Quindlen gets a *frisson* out of attending Midnight Mass at Christmas and thinks it probable that she will want a priest at her deathbed. So she is a "Catholic."

The fact that Catholicism (or any orthodox faith) has never understood itself in quotation marks does not bother Ms. Quindlen. Nor does the possibility that there might be such a thing as objective truth entailing a faith which makes demands. Kantian subjectivity is the norm here as everywhere; the isolated consciousness as the ultimate arbiter (Rilke's image of modern man as a panther silently gazing from its cage). But it's curious how the isolated consciousness, despite its vaunted independence, seldom deviates by a single degree from the prevailing secular wind.

It is perhaps not entirely Ms. Quindlen's fault, however, as her whims are catered to by parties in the Catholic Church. Similarly, Protestants can shop and choose among innumerable denominations whose ministers are attuned to the zeitgeist. Even evangelical preachers who hurl the literal word of God at their flocks like lightning bolts make a careful detour around Christ's strictures against divorce.

But as the harder theological content of faith is played down or eliminated, so is the "sign of contradiction" which the Bible speaks about. Authentic Christianity and Judaism have always been countercultural. The toning down of the less comfortable aspects of revelation is nonetheless an ongoing project in almost every denomination. A few years ago a Catholic priest in New York was accosted by a college student who told him that the pastor of her church in Brooklyn said that there is no such place as hell because a God of love could not have created it. "Is there a hell?" she asked. "Yes, there is a hell," the priest shot back. "You go back and ask your pastor how a God of love could have created Brooklyn."

So if the baby boomers want an edited version of the Sermon on the Mount (where hell is mentioned five times), they can find it in the most traditional quarters. Indeed, when they enter a church they will often find that the preachers, ecumenical committees, liturgical panels, and other such parties are way ahead of them when it comes to accommodating the spirit of the age. Innovations such as "inclusive" language in the liturgy (God as "he/she") or the declaration of a parish as a "nuclear-free zone" are far more in favor among the administrative elites than among the laity.

In these matters, it is the religious wing of the so-called New Class which usually sets the agenda. Who are these people? They are the "experts," the "issues-oriented" bureaucrats, the little wheels that spin so furiously in organizations like the World Council of Churches and the U.S. Catholic Conference. No figure is more destructive of his own and others' well-being than the man or woman who has no faith and yet makes a career of religion. But these spiritual operatives are everywhere. They tend to be hostile to normative culture, to use a vocabulary which neutralizes the traditional wisdom of language, and to cultivate a form of nihilism which is so soft and yielding that fighting it is like fighting a mist. E. M. Forster caught some of their elusive traits in a posthumous fragment called *Arctic Summer:*

> "I'll tell you about him if you like," said Mr. Vullamy
> . . . "Whitbly's the age. . . . I object to him really as a
> type which is poisonous and spreading. Poisonous is
> too strong a word for it. Every word is too strong for it

—that's the trouble . . . He's against morality—but quietly, mind you, quietly; against religion, but quietly . . . Lance's Socialist on Bramley Down is open: we know where we are with him . . . [But Whitbly] fights no one. His aim is to modify, till everything's slack and lukewarm. . . . And when he has modified, then the real forces of evil—of which he has no conception— then they'll come in and take their turn."

The Whitblys of the religious establishment apply the word "evil" only to political arrangements of which they disapprove. They scoff at the notion of sin, but find plenty of guilt—so long as it, too, remains a political category. ("I am a white male chauvinist.") Make any reference to the harder truths of revelation and they will accuse you of being rigid and authoritarian. The only absolutes they believe in are plurality (i.e., the absolute relativity of the absolute) and freedom of expression—as long as certain liberal taboos aren't violated. (Even nihilism, as Saul Bellow observed, has its no-nos.) They seldom attack traditional religion directly, but seek rather to create a soft, undermining atmosphere in which it becomes finally unintelligible.

In America, the religious New Class is in alliance with secularists who share the same political agenda but would go further in emasculating religion. The ace in the hole of the latter group is the establishment clause of the First Amendment. They have succeeded to the point where the teaching centers of American life are no longer "neutral," as far as the believing Jew or Christian is concerned, but increasingly hostile. The American Civil Liberties Union, which functions as the legal arm of secular humanism, would like to remove religion, even as a private referent, from the public arena. To this end, it sent an agent to follow Congressman Henry Hyde into church on Sunday in order to argue that Hyde's position on abortion was invalid because it derived from his Catholic faith.

But the notion that religion must never intrude on public

life is purely a product of the secular forces unleashed by the Reformation. There is no such thing as a strictly private religion in either the Old or New Testaments, where the emphasis is entirely on a "community of believers." If anyone in the Bible had an excuse for following his own private light, it was Saint Paul after his experience on the road to Damascus. But he put himself under the tutelage of the early Church. The idea that the metaphysical grounding of one's behavior is strictly a personal matter, like a taste for cigars, was contested by, of all people, the comedian Jackie Gleason. Concerning his reluctance to part with Roman Catholicism, which he no longer practiced, Gleason once remarked to a reporter from *Time*:

> Whenever I hear someone say that religion is their own personal affair, I am irritated. Religion can't be called personal. The health of your religion determines the compassion, sympathy, forgiveness, and tolerance you give to your fellow man. I have studied different religions to see if there was one more attractive for me. I only discovered I was seeking a religion that was more compatible to my way of thinking. I remained a Catholic. It wasn't comfortable, but what religion is to a sinner? While I might not carry out my obligations in any manner to be commended, at least I know where I stand.

But most baby boomers prefer not to know exactly where they stand. They are comfortable with a vague, elastic faith that expands to fill the world after a pleasant Christmas service and contracts to nothing when confronted with difficulties. In the strange and lurid atmosphere of American popular culture, this soft religious glow can take odd forms. I was in Memphis on the tenth anniversary of Elvis Presley's death. Pilgrims had arrived from all over; there was an all-night candle vigil outside the gates of Presley's home, Graceland, while all day crowds filed past the tombstone in the "Meditation Garden." Graceland has become the Lourdes of North America. I listened on the radio to a young woman saying that when she could not sleep at night, she talked to Elvis. Flannery O'Connor remarked that the modern South is "Christ-haunted," but it can safely be said that lower middle-class whites of Dixie are Elvis-haunted. It should be recalled that at the time of his death, Elvis was reading a book about the discovery of Jesus's skeleton.

I don't think this sort of thing goes on in Europe. In Europe, you're either in the Church or (more likely) out of it. There is less room for spiritual whimsy. But anything goes on this side of the Atlantic. A twenty-year-old girl from Indiana with whom I once discussed religion told me that she had a great respect for it because at camp one of the other girls was a witch who slipped off into the woods and set up an altar to worship Nature and "it was really quite beautiful." Shiva Naipaul, the late British journalist, toured America at the end of the '70s and was appalled at the free-floating spirituality. The sheer innocence of the natives' quest for various gestalts and *satori* made him think of the race of Eloi in H. G. Wells's *The Time Machine*, who play and fashion garlands while the ravenous Morlocks plan supper below.

Thomas Mann had a less disarming version of the Eloi that fits the current American situation like a glove. In the pivotal chapter of *The Magic Mountain*, the good bourgeois Hans Castorp dreams of an Arcadian landscape where beautiful human creatues dance and sport in the foam, a place where "reasoned goodness conditions every act." Soon, though, Castorp is drawn to a solemn temple which somehow seems at the heart of the matter. With increasing apprehension, he penetrates the sanctuary of the temple; there he finds two gray old women "with hanging breasts and dugs of finger-length" dismembering a small child.

We have not had the universal collapse of values which Nietzsche predicted would happen when the radical consciousness of the death of God took hold in the Western mind. There is still in America an ethical mood that feeds on the Judeo-Christian tradition. "Niceness" is the public mode here, just as phlegmatic indifference is in England. But the temptation is to regard ourselves as being as good as our public manner. In America today, you can hold on to your isolated selfishness, you can be cold and egotistical in the more hidden channels of daily life, you can dismiss the 1.6 million children aborted each year as the private affair of others, all the while keeping intact a vague righteousness which can be turned up like a thermostat whenever a nicely choreographed moment of injustice occurs on the evening news.

But even in the area of moral decorum, cracks are appearing. For example, on Wall Street, which is the epicenter of yuppiedom, there has been an extraordinary decline of moral standards. I am not referring to the occasional scoundrel caught by the SEC, but to the whole mode of doing business. The generation of bankers now retiring had a severe understanding of the word "trust" and of what constitutes a conflict of interest. It was virtually precoded in their genes. But young investment bankers today think nothing of writing fairness opinions for corporate buyouts they know are neither fair to the shareholders nor good for the public, as long as they pocket their million-dollar fee.

On Wall Street, as elsewhere, the baby boomers substitute legalisms for morality. The current plague of litigation is an obvious result of the decline of spiritual consensus. With everyone cultivating his own private judgment about what is right and wrong, issues that used to be resolved by universal preconscious assent are now turned over to the courts. Thirty years ago, the question of whether a woman can keep a baby she has carried to term as her side of a legal arrangement known as "surrogate motherhood" would never have reached the courts because it would never occur to anybody to draw up such a heartless contract in the first place.

I don't want to go on about the signs of spiritual exhaustion in this country. The republic will probably muddle on in its engaging innocence. Was it a Frenchman who said that God looks after drunks, small children, and the United States of America? Our still-solid bourgeois world nonetheless puts one in mind of the aging Charlemagne who made a journey along the Atlantic coast and saw the Viking sails slipping by against the horizon like black birds. He began to weep, clearly aware of the dangers that were to swamp the West after his death. America has thus far enjoyed a dispensation from the meat grinder of what most people at most times have experienced as history. One wonders what will happen if the country is ever caught in its gruesome machinery. *The New York Times Magazine* and other journals discover a return to traditional religion every decade or so, but it will take an unprecedented cataclysm, a new Dark Ages, to turn back the tide of a secularism which so often appropriates a religious vocabulary for its own ends.

The Drunks Shall Inherit the Earth

Susan Vigilante

A thirty-five-year-old friend of mine was telling me about his experiences in a "twelve-step" program, one of the many programs for people recovering from addictions of all sorts that are based on the principles of Alcoholics Anonymous. He talked about how he had worked his way through the steps. "I got to the point where I had to try to make amends to the people I had wronged," he said. "I thought: Oh, God, I can't possibly do this. Everyone I have to talk to already thinks I'm a jerk. What are they going to think when I call them from out of the blue and try to apologize?" He winced at the memory. "It was really tough. I felt like such an ass. But I thought, at least I'm getting it off my chest. And I knew it was the right thing to do.

"For the most part, everyone I called was pretty decent to me, which I can tell you isn't exactly what I was expecting. Then I got to the call I'd been dreading most—this girl I used to know. I hadn't spoken to her in a couple of years. I had borrowed a lot of money from her, mostly to pay for my addictions, and then I just disappeared, dropped out of her life—and, incidentally, never paid her back.

"I almost didn't call her. But my sponsor in the program said to me: 'Listen, just how important do you think you are to these people? You're not the center of their lives, you know. As far as they're concerned, you're just a shithead. So if you think this is going to be the most important phone call they ever get, that's your pride talking.' So I called her. And I made amends."

He leaned forward in his chair. "You know what she said? She said, 'Gosh, John, I used to think you were just a self-centered jerk. But now . . . I have a lot of respect for you now." He sat back and smiled at me. "It made me feel like a million bucks."

◆

If you want to take the pulse of American life without hiring a pollster, go to the checkout stand of the nearest grocery store and look at the magazine racks. The first thing you're likely to see are the tabloids, the gaudy weeklies that chronicle the sins of the stars. You won't have to read very far in them to discover that the fast track has been slowing down a lot lately. Devotees of the gossip columns know that hardly a day goes by without another actor, director, or producer checking into Betty Ford. A recent issue of *People*, the white-collar edition of the *National Enquirer*, contained an article about the low-key life-styles of Hollywood's younger stars, who reportedly favor staying home and watching TV over going out to trendy nightclubs and partying until the sun comes up. Mentioned in passing is the fact that one of the favored restaurants of these youthful luminaries is around the corner from the place where one of Los Angeles' better-attended Alcoholics Anonymous meetings is held. The title of an article that appeared in *Mademoiselle* not long ago sums it all up: "Addiction Chic."

One word that turns up regularly in such articles is "rehab," a popular shorthand term for "rehabilitation." People who talk of "being in rehab" are referring to clinics to which alcoholics and drug addicts are admitted for detoxification and several weeks of rigorous residential therapy, at the end of which they are strongly encouraged to attend A.A. meetings every day for several months. More generally, they are referring to the "rehab culture": the society of people who suffer from some form of addiction and who have dealt with it by joining A.A. or some other twelve-step program. The use of the word "culture" begins to make more sense when you consider the vast numbers of people who fill this bill. *Mademoiselle* claims that "there are an estimated 12 to 15 million people—up from 5 to 8 million in 1976 —currently involved in about 500,000 organizations" that seek to treat various kinds of addictions.

A useful index of the size of the rehab culture is the way in which the publishing industry is catering to its needs. *The New York Times Book Review* looked into the rehab phenomenon earlier this year and found that one publisher, Harper & Row, which collaborates with the Hazelden Foundation, an offshoot of the prestigious Hazelden Clinic, on a special line of "recovery" books, had about eighty such titles in print, many of which make explicit use of twelve-step ideas and techniques. One Harper/ Hazelden title, Melody Beattie's *Codependent No More*, had been on the *Times* best-seller list for seventy weeks and sold about 1,500,000 copies (it's still selling). Another publishing house that specializes in recovery books has over one hundred titles in print, one of which, Janet G. Woititz's *Adult Children of Alcoholics*, has sold over a million copies to date. Then, of course, there are the "official" publications of the rehab culture, the books and pamphlets published by A.A. and its related fellowships and sold to members at meetings or by mail. *Alcoholics Anonymous*, the handbook of A.A., as well as such other fellowships as Overeaters Anonymous, is in its thirty-third printing, with an estimated 4 million copies in print; *One Day at a Time*, the Al-Anon book of daily meditations, has passed its nineteenth printing.

Who is buying all these books? You don't have to read the *National Enquirer* to get a sneaking feeling that the rehab culture consists mostly of baby boomers. Look at the numbers. If it's true that the number of participants in twelve-step and related programs has doubled since 1976, it's clearly a safe bet that a substantial part of the increase can be attributed to dramatically increased participation by baby boomers, the oldest of whom turned thirty in 1976, a good age to start thinking about getting clean and sober.

Besides, it makes sense. As my friend the former self-centered jerk would be the first to tell you, the baby boom generation contains more than its fair share of self-centered jerks. By "jerks," I mean people who are egotistical, insensitive, and rude; greedy climbers whose only aim in life is to advance their own careers, reputations, and tax brackets, preferably stepping on as many other people as possible on the way; people who want to turn the Me Decade into a lifetime commitment. In other words, people who resemble the stock TV image of the Very Successful Baby Boomer. (Scene: a fancy health-club locker room. Enter a sweaty young-exec type. He storms into the room, rips off his T-shirt, glares into the camera and snaps: "I give a hundred and ten percent, and *I expect it!*")

We have all met people like this, maybe even too many of them. How many baby boomers are like this is open to dispute, and how they came to be that way is a subject of endless debate. They were spoiled by liberalism, ruined by Reaganism. They were mugged by the public schools, cosseted by the private schools, spoiled by indulgent parents, brutalized by harsh ones. They were twisted by the recession of the '70s or the bull market of the '80s. Or maybe it was Dr. Spock. Or Dr. Freud. Or Dr. Ruth. Whatever the reason, and however exaggerated their numbers and their awfulness have been, I think there is no getting around the unpleasant truth that far too many baby boomers suffer from chronic spiritual malnutrition. It's not that we're any worse than anyone else; it's just that serious moral and spiritual training have not been particularly high on the national agenda lately. The high incidence of jerkism is proof of that. So is the fact that my generation has also apparently produced a bumper crop of cokeheads, dope fiends, drunks and all sorts of other addicts of all varieties: gambling addicts, sex addicts, even food addicts. Right along with them come the hordes of "codependents," people who may not be addicts themselves but whose lives have been made a lot worse by the addicts they are married to, related to, in love with, or otherwise associated with. The overlap between the addicts and codependents on one hand and the jerks on the other is, to put it mildly, considerable.

But there is a light at the end of the tunnel: hundreds of thousands of addicts and their codependents are now marching straight into rehab programs. Even more importantly, they are also joining the various twelve-step programs that are the lifetime followup to rehab, and on which much of rehab theory is based.

I am not, thank God, an addict. But like everyone else in New York (or so it sometimes seems), I have a number of addicted people in my life: friends, associates, relatives. At the invitation of a friend, I started going to Al-Anon meetings five years ago. Al-Anon, like the other "Anon" groups, is for people who have alcoholics in their lives and who develop their own distinctive sets of problems as a result. (In fact, some say the codependent is an alcoholic without the bottle. One evening I went to a midtown Manhattan church that was hosting both an A.A. meeting and an Al-Anon meeting. I went up to the two well-dressed, thirtyish people who were greeting newcomers at the door of one room, which turned out to be the A.A. meeting. Feeling somewhat sheepish, I explained, "I was looking for Al-Anon." "Oh," they replied in cheery chorus, "you want the Almost Alcoholics meeting!")

Over the past five years, I've talked to a lot of people in a lot of programs. Although twelve-step programs have members of all ages, most of the people I've gotten to know through them are, like me, baby boomers. It has become increasingly clear to me that these people are doing much more than learning how to overcome their various addictions. They are also learning how to overcome the characteristic disease of their generation: they are learning how not to be jerks.

. . .

The rehab culture, not surprisingly, is leaving its mark on the work of a growing number of younger film and TV writers and directors. The principal characters of the popular NBC television series "Cheers" (Sam Malone) and "Hill Street Blues" (Capt. Frank Furillo) were portrayed as recovering alcoholics. Michael Keaton, lately of *Batman* fame, played a fast-track, cocaine-addicted baby boom businessman forced into rehab in the 1988 film *Clean and Sober*, directed by Glenn Gordon Caron, creator of the ABC series "Moonlighting." Actress Carrie Fisher's delightful autobiographical novel *Postcards from the Edge*, a tale of addiction and recovery, has just been made into a film. I suspect that the main reason Hollywood is beginning to make use of rehab-related themes is because so many entertainment professionals, most of them baby boomers, have themselves gone into rehab programs for drug and alcohol addiction. Wherever they go, they are being introduced to the Twelve Steps (usually through A.A.) and urged to continue attending twelve-step meetings after they check out.

One consequence of this increased media exposure is a growing awareness in the larger culture of the external trappings of programs like A.A. Not so long ago, bumper stickers that read "One Day at a Time" or "Keep It Simple" were a mystery to the average motorist; now there's a good chance that they will be recognized as A.A. slogans and the driver thereby identified as a member of A.A. or a related fellowship. For those who aren't familiar with the mechanics of an A.A. meeting, however, a short description may be helpful.

The typical twelve-step meeting is held in a church basement, or some other place decorated by the same firm of interior decorators that holds the church basement monopoly: a village hall, say, or a hospital conference room. You walk into a roomful of folding chairs that have been set up in neat and (in New York, anyway) rather closely packed rows. At the front of the room there is a little table with two chairs, one for the chairman and one for the speaker of the evening. The chairman starts the meeting by introducing himself and reading a standard greeting. Then he introduces the speaker. The speaker, who is often a regular member of the particular group, will tell the group something about himself and about his own experiences "in program." He may talk about some specific aspect of the program, perhaps even about one or more of the Twelve Steps, which are usually listed on a poster hanging on a wall somewhere in the room.

After ten or fifteen minutes, the speaker opens the meeting to the group. What happens next? Not much—at least not on the face of it. People talk. They raise their hands and then they say something. They may comment on the speaker's talk, or talk about their own struggle with addiction. They may tell the group about what a rotten day they had, or what a good day they had. Sometimes they say something funny and the whole group laughs. Sometimes they burst into tears, and then the other members simply listen in silence as their fellow sufferer cries.

The underlying principle at work in an A.A. meeting is bound to seem inexplicable to outsiders. How can simply talking to a roomful of strangers help you to get your life together? As a counselor at one rehab clinic told me, "It's the sharing that does the healing." On the surface, that kind of statement sounds like a bunch of touchy-feely nonsense, a throwback to the communal excesses of the '60s; it also bears a superficial resemblance to the jargon of the self-actualization and New Age movements. Many observers, particularly liberal rationalists who bristle with hostility at any open manifestation of religious or quasireligious belief, traditional or otherwise, are put off by this resemblance. Wendy Kaminer, writing about the literature of codependency for *The New York Times Book Review*, complains about the "relentless optimism" of the self-help movement and goes so far as to argue that "codependency and other self-help books discourage independent thought. . . . Self-help books market authority in a culture that idealizes individualism but not thinking and fears the isolation of being free."

This kind of criticism misses the point of the twelve-step

philosophy, which is rooted in a conception of human nature profoundly at odds with the shallow optimism of self-actualization. Self-actualization is about "fulfilling your unique and infinite potential as a human being." A twelve-step fellowship is about facing up to your very ordinary failures as a human being, in the company of people who have failed just as much and are willing to admit it without indulging in that special form of pride known as despair. The self-actualization movement promises to put you in control of your life; twelve-step programs teach the obvious if neglected truth that you never were in control of your life, and a good thing, too. The self-actualization movement teaches that falls aren't for guys like me; the twelve-step fellowships, drawing on more ancient wisdom, teach that pride goeth before a fall. In fact, in a twelve-step program, you learn that the fall is the good part, the first step on a spiritual journey you might not otherwise have taken.

The key word here is, of course, "spiritual." At the end of every twelve-step meeting, everyone in the room stands up and joins hands. Those who wish to recite the Serenity Prayer together: *God grant me the serenity to accept the things I cannot change, the courage to change the things I can, and the wisdom to know the difference.* Then they grip each other's hands a little more firmly and say in unison, "Keep coming back. It works if you work it." What "works" for them is the program, the most essential component of which is the Twelve Steps.

The steps were composed by Bill Wilson, one of the two founders of A.A. and himself a prototypical "yuppie" of the '30s, a fast-talking, fast-track margins dealer whose life went to hell via the booze route. All the twelve-step programs—Gamblers Anonymous, Overeaters Anonymous, and the others—use essentially the same steps, substituting their particular addiction (or codependency) for alcohol. I list the steps as Wilson composed them below, but I invite the reader to substitute the addiction of his choice:

1. We admitted we were powerless over alcohol—that our lives had become unmanageable.

2. Came to believe that a Power greater than ourselves could restore us to sanity.

3. Made a decision to turn our will and our lives over to the care and direction of God *as we understood Him.*

4. Made a searching and fearless moral inventory of ourselves.

5. Admitted to God, to ourselves, and to another human being the exact nature of our wrongs.

6. Were entirely ready to have God remove all these defects of character.

7. Humbly asked Him to remove our shortcomings.

8. Made a list of all persons we had harmed, and became willing to make amends to them all.

9. Made direct amends to such people wherever possible, except when to do so would injure them or others.

10. Continued to take personal inventory and when we were wrong promptly admitted it.

11. Sought through prayer and meditation to improve our conscious contact with God as we understood Him, praying only for knowledge of His will for us and the power to carry that out.

12. Having had a spiritual awakening as the result of these steps, we tried to carry this message to others, and to practice these principles in all our affairs.

Perhaps the most striking aspect of the Twelve Steps is the fact that they refer so frequently and explicitly to God and to the need for recovering alcoholics to undergo a "spiritual awakening." As it happens, neither of the two men who founded A.A. was religious in any conventional sense. (Bill Wilson called himself an agnostic.) Twelve-steppers tend not to talk about religion very much; at some meetings, it is considered positively *déclassé* to use the term. While much of their official literature freely uses the word "God," many twelve-steppers talk instead about their "Higher Power." Pressed to define this "Higher Power," many will admit they mean God—that is, the Big Guy in the Old and New Testaments—though others insist that they mean something or someone much less specific, like nature, or perhaps the "group consciousness" of their particular twelve-step fellowship. But they will all talk about "spirituality." To them, recovery is more than just a matter of getting clean and sober. It entails renewal of spirit, the attainment of a new way of looking at oneself and one's life. Without such renewal, the twelve-stepper believes, recovery is at best short-term and disappointing.

The kind of "spiritual awakening" to which the twelve steps refer is precisely the kind of awakening that is desperately needed by the average baby boomer. Baby boomers, secularized ones in particular, like to believe that they're in total control of their lives. Small wonder. That's precisely what they were told, over and over again, from childhood onward; that's what today's "self-help" movement, whose very name indicates how little it has in common with the Twelve Steps, is telling them now. Your local bookstore is crammed to the eyeballs with paperbacks promising that all you have to do is believe in yourself and your life will be wonderful. Pop psychology tomes like *I'm OK, You're OK* and *When I Say No, I Feel Guilty* were the Little Red Books of the '70s and '80s; I have vivid memories of seminars in high school that preached the virtues of "taking charge of your life" and cultivating "a positive self-image." (And I went to a religious school!)

Thanks to years of relentless propagandizing, many baby boomers find it extremely galling to admit that it takes something outside of themselves to save them, to admit that after all the successes and honors and degrees, they still cannot manage their own lives without recourse to a Higher Power. This resistance is based on one of the most powerful of all human failings: pride.

The baby boomers were suckled on pride. Ten years of the Me Decade and another ten of the Roaring '80s produced enough fertilizer to turn seedling-sized egos into something like the killer plant in *Little Shop of Horrors*. The time has come for these man-eaters to take a long, hard look at themselves. The purpose of the Twelve Steps is to facilitate the taking of just such looks. Honesty is what the Twelve Steps are all about. If such honesty "discourages independent thought," then maybe independent thought, at least as defined by people like Wendy Kaminer, isn't quite all it's cracked up to be.

I read in *The New York Times* the other day that a growing number of prominent religious leaders, disturbed by the shrinking sizes of their congregations and impressed by the growing visibility and apparent effectiveness of twelve-step programs, were looking into the possibility of making use of twelve-step techniques. I'm not surprised. The influence of A.A., Al-Anon, and other twelve-step programs is not confined to the members of the programs themselves, or even to their families and other codependents. Indeed, I have come to believe that the twelve-step fellowships may turn out to be the most powerful and significant spiritual movement of our day—particularly for the baby boomers.

Bear in mind that A.A. is only about two generations old, while the other twelve-step programs are even younger. As a result, the baby boomers are really the first generation for which such programs have been widely available, which is singularly appropriate when you remember that we were the ones who turned the abuse of the sorts of substances that make people eligible for these programs into a generational ritual. It's true that there have always been plenty of drunks and other addicts around. But the universality of the vice does nothing to diminish the fact that a frighteningly large percentage of baby boomers have tried to "enrich" their lives with booze and drugs and sex and an unholy host of other cheap thrills and have ended up nearly destroying those lives in the process.

What makes the drunks and addicts and codependents of the baby boom so different? The fact that we were bred to success has a lot to do with it. We grew up in a time of real, if fluctuating, prosperity, and many roads that were closed to our parents and grandparents were wide open to us. (Blacks in the Ivy League! Women in the boardrooms! Conservatives in the White House!) The world of the youthful baby boomer was one of endless possibilities. But addicts are not the only failures this generation will produce. Who among us will never lose money, or invest it badly, sooner or later? Whose first (or second, or third) book will not be rejected, or panned, or simply ignored? Whose child will not have trouble in school, or in society? We have reached an age when disasters start to happen to people like us with increasing regularity. We have begun at last to notice that we are not, after all, perfect.

Perhaps we knew that all along. Perhaps our most private dreams have been fantasies of simple acceptance: acceptance without benefit of resumé, without a long list of stellar achievements, without a nicely invested portfolio and a perfect apartment and a drop-dead automobile. Perhaps that is why so many of us are turning to the twelve-step fellowships, which teach that you are acceptable, warts and all; that everyone else is acceptable, too; that in learning to tolerate the weaknesses of others, you learn to tolerate yourself. These fellowships are taking baby boomers who have wrecked their lives and turning them into an invaluable social asset: an advance guard of spirituality for a generation that knows nothing of the spirit.

It has been a long time since any generation has been as systematically deprived of, even deliberately cut off from, the kind of spiritual training that the Twelve Steps offer. By now, many of us have come to suspect that we are missing something, missing a vital part of ourselves, the part we thought would make us brave and honest and true. Every one of us has to find that part; the Twelve Steps are a proven place to start looking. Alcoholics and drug addicts are not the only ones who need spiritual renewal. We all do. It is in large part because of the Twelve Steps that some of us are getting it at last. Are the baby boomers a generation of jerks? Perhaps. But for every baby boomer who enters a twelve-step program and sticks with it, the number of jerks drops by one. And that is a good thing for all of us.

House Lust
(and Other Sexual Perversions
of the Baby Boom Era)

Maggie Gallagher

*I*t happened again. Tuesday morning. 10:30 a.m. I was all alone. Just me, a cup of Egyptian cappuccino and a copy of *The New York Times*. Then I saw it. My heart leaped to my throat and began some peculiar gyrations in that narrow space. Underneath the table, my toes started tap, tap, tapping against the floor.

It was just a classified ad. Two staid lines of type in the staid old newspaper: *Pk. Slp. Handyman special: $189,900.*

My whole body was getting into the rhythm now. My lungs informed me that they needed quick, panting action. My stomach pretended it was hungry. Then my intestines picked up the tune and started to bump and grind. It was the most amazing combination of anticipation and anxiety, an intensely physical yearning for a gratification tap dancing ever farther beyond one's grasp, a sort of Disco Blues. I had the symptoms down cold by now. Oh, yes, I knew what it meant. Here it was again: my old friend House Lust.

What is house lust, you might ask? If you have to ask, you must be either over forty or too young to vote. House lust is an epileptic fit of frustrated desire that occurs when the price of the average house rises to more than four times the amount of the average income, when you come to realize that you will never again achieve the standard of living you had in junior high school. In 1963, the median price for a home was $18,000. Today it is $120,000. Even adjusted for inflation, that's an increase of 72%. In 1973, 43.6% of twenty-five- to twenty-nine-year-olds owned their own homes. In 1987, only 35.9% could afford a home of their own. Meanwhile, homeownership among sixty-four- to seventy-five-year-olds grew by almost 10% over the same period. In my case, house lust is what you get when you call a realtor about a $189,900 handyman special advertised in the morning paper and discover it's just been sold for $200,000. Among the younger baby boomers, house lust has reached epidemic proportions.

This is an age of mobility. I had two childhood homes. My parents don't live in either of them anymore. The first was a big colonial in a nice Catholic neighborhood in Portland, Oregon, called Laurelhurst. It had a big, cheery kitchen, a round break-fast nook, a formal dining room, a screened porch, a living room with fireplace, a den that belonged to my father, a finished basement with a built-in closet under the staircase that served as our secret hideout, two bathrooms, and four bedrooms upstairs, each with its own rickety balcony my mother refused to let us play on. My favorite parts were the laundry chute on the second floor, which we used to pass secret messages to the basement and give thrill rides to reluctant teddy bears, and the large, lush magnolia tree in the front yard next to a forest of rhododendron. It dropped huge teardrop seedpods covered with a five o'clock shadow of prickles on which I first practiced the art of barbering. When I was eight, the family moved to a glorified ranch house in the suburbs, which had an even bigger yard, two kitchens, three family rooms, four bathrooms, six bedrooms, and a lake.

I am luckier than most people.

I now live in Brooklyn, which many people (not including my mother) consider a nice compromise between Manhattan's

Upper East Side and Portland, Oregon. I live in a delightful family` neighborhood where delightful family brownstones are considered delightfully reasonably priced at $500,000.

Yes, I am one of the lucky ones, blessed with a warm, generous family, an Ivy League education, and a potentially prestigious career as a journalist. I am supposed to be grateful for all the advantages I have, but I am not. I am petulant and bad-tempered. I rebel against my fate. I am twenty-nine years of age, seven years out of college, and I live with my son in a two-room apartment with twelve-foot decorative tin ceilings and cracks in the walls.

My son, Patrick, who is six, gives me lectures in housing. "This apartment is old," he tells me. "The walls are old, the floors are old, it is *disgusting*," he says definitively, pausing for a moment while I digest this information in silence. Then he goes on: "I want to live in a house with a slanted roof and a chimney, on the first floor, which has only *o–n–e family* living in it, in a nice neighborhood with lots of grass and trees."

I'm listening to Patrick with one ear. The other is trained on a handsome middle-aged gentleman at a party at the Irish consulate who is telling me what is wrong with baby boomers. "Your generation expects too much," he tells me, his voice booming good-naturedly. He has a kind, jovial face and almost-white hair. About fifty-five, I would guess. About my father's age. "You have more affluence than most generations in American history."

He is from a generation that lived through the Depression (as children) and the Second World War (as teenagers) and therefore feels entitled forevermore to lecture others about Hard Times and Doing Without. His generation, which came of age during the greatest continuous period of affluence in American history, got college educations, bought houses, could afford children and full-time mothers, and didn't have to pay 14% of its income off the top in Social Security.

Baby boomers have been called shallow, greedy, money-hungry. We carry too much debt and not enough diapers. All this is true. But today, for the first time in history, the young are seven times more likely to be poor than the old. When pilgrims came to virgin land seeking a better life, when our parents' generation fled to suburbs carved out of potato fields of Long Island where for a hundred down and a hundred a month they could have the American dream, they were not called such nasty names as we, moving into old, decaying, crime-infested neighborhoods, trying to carve out a middle-class life-style for our children, seeking a piece of land, the stability of a permanent neighborhood, a piece of the pie, a house of our own.

We of the baby boom generation are yuppies. We commit gentrification and other heinous sins. Then we dress up in sack-cloth and ashes, beat our breasts and confess in great anguished voices, "Yes, yes, I did it! I took an old decaying brownstone shell and fixed it up real nice! And then (sob) I got involved in the public school and made it safe for my children! And after that, I cleaned up the streets, brought new businesses into the neighborhood—and, and, I am so ashamed!" To expiate our sins, we deny our yuppiehood and refuse to allow anyone else to ruin another neighborhood like we did. What is a yuppie, anyway? A young upwardly mobile professional. Did we really need a new word to describe young people who want to get ahead?

But this is the age of the acronym. We make up new terms to describe all the diverse and perverse life-styles we fervently pursue. One enterprising market analyst has coined dozens of neologisms to describe various social niches (a social niche being defined as a group of people who buy the same product) and tracked us down to the zip codes in which we live. Take "Urban Gold Coast," for example. Members of this niche may be over sixty-five or under twenty-four, but two thirds live in residences worth more than $200,000. They buy imported champagne, but not cars. When they go to the grocery store, they stock up on orange juice, English muffins, and yogurt. Manhattan is full of Urban Gold Coasters. Other niches, with equivalent amounts of disposable income, spend their money quite differently, like "Furs and Station Wagons" (Needham, Massachusetts, is an example) or "Pools and Patios" (single-family houses filled with aging empty-nesters who enjoy domestic champagne, health clubs, and subscriptions to *Sunset* and *The Wall Street Journal*). "Levittown U.S.A." is much like "Pools and Patios," but with cheaper houses and fewer college degrees. Levittowners bowl. They also buy new roofs, golf equipment, instant iced tea and subscriptions to *Stereo Review*. "Hispanic Mix" buys asthma remedies but not dental rinse. "Bohemian Mixers" buy wine by the case but not wall paneling.

This is the new America. Tribalism runs amok. It is, come to think of it, the same kind of tribalism we got used to in high school, where gang members wore the same jacket, jocks put on the same uniforms, and cliques of high-heeled girls smoked the same brand of cigarettes.

In a tribal society, people have many enemies. Mine are the DINKS: Double Income, No Kids. They live in my neighborhood. They come in droves from Manhattan, driving up real estate prices, occupying valuable space in one of the few public school districts in New York City you can send your kid to with an (almost) clear conscience. Apartments with backyards become "garden floor-throughs" so their English cocker spaniel has a place to do his doo-doo. My son's nerfball, bouncing off the walls, is a tomtom beating in my blood, a call to battle. But DINKS are bigger and stronger and have more money than I do, and their hands are not tied down with lunchboxes and baseball gloves and they do not trip over tiny pink plastic dinosaurs when they walk through their apartments, so I pass up the opportunity for open warfare. They will live to eat sun-dried tomatoes another day. Discretion is the better part of bathos, and besides, this is a family neighborhood. Let them live: soon, perhaps a little bundle of joy will grace their Art Deco pad. Then they will become DIKS, and that will be revenge enough.

I have made up a new acronym myself. It describes people

like me: PUPS, Poor Urban Professionals. The distinguishing feature of the current age is not the materialistic upward mobility of yuppies but our downward mobility, which the frantic pursuit of the perfect pair of shoes disguises. The rise in housing prices and the decline in the quality of public schools has produced a new class of the proletariat composed of college-educated men and women (especially women) who cannot sustain a middle-class standard of living for their children. In the teeming metropolis, we exist in droves. We have excellent taste. We have prestigious jobs in artsy professions. We simply cannot afford to educate or house our children in the manner to which we once hoped they would become accustomed. We are the latest impoverished gentility, huddling around empty blocked-up hearths in nineteenth-century flats, cultivating our knowledge of fashion trends, the most exclusive nightclubs and the best bars of soap as tokens of our faded social standing.

New York City is a place driven by class hatred. The poor hate the rich and the rich hate the poor. And both of them together conspire against the middle class. The consequence of this conspiracy is that the middle class is pretty much gone from the city now. Everyone is poor here, unless they strike it rich. It is not polite to mention this fact in public. Certainly politicians never do. The rest of us seldom admit it either, even to ourselves. But there it remains, lurking in the hearts of men, awaiting only the right opportunity to bare its ugly fangs and strike.

And nothing bares this class hatred like shopping for houses. If you are a PUP seeking a house for your family, you have two choices. You can drive through the burned-out shells of neighborhoods that forty years of welfare politics have produced and commit the sin of loathing those poorer than you who live there, who have rendered so much of the American Dream unfit for human habitation. Or you can stroll through "middle-class" neighborhoods and loathe the gentry who can afford what you are permanently denied. They are the new gentry, blessed by birth. Perhaps they literally inherited the family estate when Aunt Mamie died in 1985. Or they were lucky enough to be born by the year 1952 and so be in a position to buy a house before prices skyrocketed in the '80s.

There is no sin less attractive than envy, or more irresistible than lust. House lust combines the worst elements of both. Oh, it is a sin all right, a stain against the soul. But people who live in glass apartments shouldn't throw stones. I am one of the guilty ones.

House lust is humbling. It thrusts one into permanent exile, wandering, itinerant, homeless, excluded: not under- but out-classed. House lust is responsible for a variety of secondary neu-roses ranging from Fastfoodophobia (stemming from a repressed desire to possess an eat-in kitchen) to the more common Status Anxiety. Let me give you an example. A young woman with a Yale degree, a six-year-old son, and a job as an editor at a maga-zine moves into a grubby apartment in Park Slope. While picking up her son at kindergarten, she makes friends with a nice black woman whose son is in the same class. The young Yale grad feels a warm glow of liberal condescension. Her son and this poor black child play side by side in peace and harmony, just like Dr. King hoped. Her small spark of condescension bursts into flames and warms her soul. How nice and liberal she is not to mind that her son plays with ghetto children.

On closer acquaintance, however, she discovered that this nice black woman is a dental hygienist from Jamaica who owns a large four-story limestone just around the corner from her own grubby little apartment with the twelve-foot tin ceilings and cracks in the walls. The nice black woman and her husband bought this house in 1978 for approximately $40,000 and it would now cost more than ten times that amount. The young woman is thrown into existential panic. Who is patronizing whom? Does an Ivy League degree equal a dental-hygiene certif-icate and a half-million-dollar limestone townhouse with marble fireplaces, or does it not? Socially speaking, it was unclear to me—um, I mean, to her. Hence the unresolved and unresolvable anxiety. A new social scale is being erected, and when the dust clears in a generation or so, only then will we finally discover whether we were upwardly or downwardly mobile.

In New York City, the great speculative housing boom appears to be over. Housing prices are climbing at a rate a little below that of inflation, while co-op prices are actually dropping. Manhattan's disease has migrated to Los Angeles and San Francisco and is radiating outward toward formerly affordable cities like Seattle. But here, there is now a breathing space in which to accumulate sufficient capital to purchase a living space. Here there is for the first time in years hope for the homeless baby boomers. But here also is the haunting fear that now, after years of saving and scrimping, when we actually do buy a home we will end up losing all our money on it. Younger boomers are buying into an inflated market and will end up selling in the deflating baby buster era. But that won't prevent us from putting all our nest eggs in one basket. Fear alone has never been sufficient to contain lust.

House lust is not an isolated phenomenon, nor is it primarily an economic one. It has its roots deep in our sexual natures, and the sudden epidemic of this desire explains and contains all the many ruptures in our sexual constitution. Slice house lust and you lay bare the angst of an age.

For women, baby lust and house lust are closely related. A house is the place to make a family. A family is the people you make a home for. A house, a hearth, a heart of our own: these are our most intimate longings. For modern women, they are also contradictory. Take my friend Colleen. At twenty-nine, she was a successful analyst for a major financial institution, footloose and fancy free, with the world at her feet and no obligations on her shoulders. But was she happy? *Noooo.* Colleen, being a smart woman, knew what she wanted: a husband, a home, a family. So with the same determination she brought to her job, she went out and acquired the first two and set about making the third. That is when the contradictions of the age turned on her and attacked. She and her husband bought their home (an unpretentious ranch house in the Jersey burbs) while she was working. Soon baby made three and her maternity leave was almost up, and while she cringed at the thought of leaving her baby, she also had a $100,000 mortgage her husband could not pay for on his salary alone. This is thoroughly a modern woman's dilemma.

For families, the much-lauded rise in family income during the Reagan era is largely a statistical illusion. Family income rose because women flooded into the workplace, working twice as hard to maintain a lower standard of living than their mothers enjoyed. Between 1959 and 1983, the collective number of hours that all women between twenty-five and sixty-four put into the marketplace nearly doubled, while the number of hours that we devoted to child care and housework decreased by only 14%. (During this same period, the combined number of hours men worked in and out of the home fell by 8%.) Yet even after the hours of a woman's workweek have almost doubled, a house of our own is slipping out of our reach. In 1967, it took 22% of the median young home-buyer's income to carry a house, while in 1987 it consumed almost a third of income. Having risen every year since the census first began tracking it after World War II, the percentage of first-time buyers who became homeowners began to drop after 1980, from 43.3% to 36.2% for twenty-five- to twenty-nine-year-olds, and from 62.4% to 52.6% for thirty- to thirty-five-year-olds.

There are many causes for this decline. The mortgage deduction actually made it cheaper for high-bracket Americans (who make more money) to buy a given home than younger boomers in lower tax brackets. And baby boomers settled down and raised families and bought houses just when communities started passing growth control laws, which vastly increased our parents' wealth while pricing us out of the market.

The demand for houses created by the bulging baby boom population pushed housing prices sky-high, out of the reach of younger baby boomers. Then, too, new kinds of households were forming rapidly. When a couple divorces, for example, two households need housing instead of only one. Singles are more likely to live on their own than with their parents, and even to buy their own houses. New life-styles increased the number of households, driving up demand and prices. Divorce, cohabitation, single households: all increased household formation.

But the epidemic of house lust is also caused by the federal government's dramatic transfer of tax burden from singles to families with children. In 1979, U.S. Treasury analyst Eugene Steuerle asked a fascinating question. Since the mid-'60s, income from the corporate income tax had fallen steadily. Single and divorced taxpayers won major tax cuts in 1969. The standard deduction for individuals had been increased several times. Congress was on the brink of reducing taxes for two-income households. Nonetheless, income-tax revenues were rising steadily. Who was paying for all this? The answer, Steuerle found, was families supporting children. Between 1960 and 1984, the average federal tax rate paid by single and childless couples remained unchanged. However, the average tax rate for a couple with two children jumped 43%. Families with four children faced a 223% increase, as inflation eroded the value of the personal deduction.

The tax code is structured to force women into paid labor by offering tax credits only to working mothers, and by the reduction of the so-called "marriage penalty." When two earners marry, they have a higher income as a couple than they did as individuals and so they are bumped into a higher tax bracket than they would be if they were merely living together. But the reduction of the "marriage penalty" for two-income families actually means that the government now taxes a traditional family which makes $40,000 more heavily than a two-earner family making the same amount. Congress reduced the "marriage penalty" by creating a "mother penalty." When married boomers require two incomes to keep a house, economic disaster becomes twice as likely to strike. If either spouse gets laid off, they may lose the house. For women without men, a middle-class life-style becomes almost impossible.

House lust contains the desire of a generation, flush with choice, for the one choice that seems beyond our reach.

We are the generation that invented choice, and we are proud of it. We crave variety in food and sex. We have regular and decaffeinated coffee, medicated or deodorant soap. We can choose tartar-control toothpaste for ourselves, and bubble-gum flavored star-shaped toothpaste with sparklies for our children. We can live alone and love it. Or we can cohabit with the person of our choice. We are single parents, gay divorcées, and married gays. Oh, yes, we can make any choice—except, increasingly, to be married and raise our children in real houses that we own, in safe neighborhoods with good schools that support and affirm for our children the moral choices we have made for ourselves.

It's not much, really. Just the American dream.

With effort, we may achieve a part of the dream. We can have a house, but we cannot afford to put children in it. Or we can have children, but we cannot give them a house in which to live. The rising cost of houses makes the housewife obsolete. Wives must work to pay the mortgage. But the lack of a housewife also makes a house obsolete because there is no time to clean it, or care for it, or wait for the repairman to fix it when it is sick, or to enjoy the children that people it. The sexual perversions of the age are transforming erotic ties into fleeting exchanges of physical sensations, marriages into momentary pacts of mutual pleasure, motherhood into something that must be squeezed in between more important commitments in the workplace.

There comes a moment when all the perversions of the age

converge. Baby boomers are hungry. Hungry for status, success, babies, homes, love, marriages, communities, wrapped up into one package: a room of one's own. A single driving desire that contains all the others: house lust.

The War Against the Yuppies

Richard Vigilante

Several years ago, I tried to launch a new magazine based on the idea that everyone is like me. Not absolutely everyone, of course. But my idea was that with nearly everyone who appeared to be like me—younger baby boomers, college-educated, urban or at least drawn to cosmopolitan culture, more or less professional—with all these people I shared common tastes, ambitions, aspirations, motives, even morals.

This might not seem like a controversial idea; in fact, I thought it rather obvious. But if I was right, one of the most powerful myths of our time, the myth of the yuppie, would have to be wrong. For if my generation really was dominated by this repulsive creature, then my colleagues, acquaintances, and friends must be very odd ducks, because there was not a yuppie among them. Could we *all* be caught in a strange warp of time and space uniquely inhospitable to these alleged creatures, while the world outside was being overrun by them? It seemed much more likely that the people I saw all around me, who seemed unexceptional in most respects, really were unexceptional, and that since (a) I had never met a yuppie and (b) almost everything one hears about them goes flatly against human nature, (c) they didn't exist.

Now it is true that none of the many categories such as

"yuppie," these evening-news, pop-sociological catchalls for a generation, a subculture, or a social plague, ever really exists. And normally it is not very interesting to go about curmudgeonously disproving their existence. People who loudly discover that real people are not sociological abstractions generally are about as interesting as children who discover hypocrisy in their elders, and should be treated the same way.

But the myth of the yuppie does seem to me worth disputing—so much so that I spent a year trying to get other people to give me several million dollars so I could dispute it full time. The yuppie myth is worth disputing not because it is false, but because it is powerful. We believe in yuppies, we hurry to distance ourselves from them, we fear becoming one. The yuppie myth has thus come to wield a considerable and destructive influence over national life, the arts and popular entertainment, and even politics.

The yuppie myth is the myth of a generation at once cynical, soulless, and self-obsessed; faultlessly fashionable, yet philistine; rootless, yet appallingly attached to material goods and overpaid for not terribly useful work, much of which includes lying, cheating, and writing obnoxious ad campaigns. We are regarded as destroyers of culture because although we are, it is supposed, obsessed with well-finished and expensive objects and willing to be seen spending money on the reportedly edifying arts, we have no genuine appreciation for creative achievement. In politics, the equation is even simpler: we are the forces of greed. On this point both left and right agree, though the left blames us for making too much money while the right thinks we make too few babies. But left or right, the accusers are usually indistinguishable from the accused. The most fervid denunciations of yuppies come from within the ranks.

I first noticed the power of the yuppie myth when I began to think about the state of the general-interest magazine market. Over the past decade, a number of publishing entrepreneurs seem to have concluded the same thing: that there is no hope that the great magazines of the past (*The New Yorker*, supremely, but *Harper's*, *The Atlantic*, and the rest as well) will make themselves an important part of the lives of the current generation. Perhaps these magazines may live to fight another day, but for now all their collective pretensions represent nothing more than a niche to be filled.

Into that niche has been launched a multitude of new (or revamped) national and regional magazines aimed squarely at the yuppies and enthusiastically supported by advertisers of liquor, fashions, and other conspicuous consumptions fairly desperate for base camps from which to hunt yuppie dollars. The new issues include titles such as *Details*, *LA Style*, *Spy*, *Vanity Fair*, such British imports as *Tatler*, and many more obscure entries. Only a minority of these are built broadly enough to fit into the old "general interest" category (*Spy*, for instance, is mostly humor), and others that might be included, such as *Metropolis* (New York architecture and interior design) or *Taxi* (mostly fashion), are even more specialized. Yet they do make up a coherent category of their own. They are "life-style" magazines. Their essential purpose is to instruct their readers in how to lead a life-style that will keep them unembarrassed, up-to-date, and fashionably busy. In the same category could reasonably be included some slightly older magazines, including the city and regional magazines such as *New York*, *Washingtonian*, and *D* (and even *Esquire* in its current incarnation), which have realized that their fortunes lie with advertisers to the yuppies.

These magazines, catering to the yuppies, are a good guide, not necessarily to who the yuppies are, but to who the publishers and the broader society *think* the yuppies are. As a group, these magazines are most remarkable for the contempt they show for their readers and for themselves. They share a common esthetic: one of nervousness. They are produced by nervous editors and art directors, in the hope of finding (or making) readers nervous enough to need the life-style advice they dispense. The editors' and art directors' nervousness shows in the pacing and the design. All these magazines encourage readers to turn the pages very quickly. Intelligible content is kept to a minimum. Often the print is oversized. "White space" is abundant and rarely white, sprinkled as it is with lots of pictures that, like the prose, are mostly there to strike an attitude.

There are apparent exceptions. *Spy* uses lots of print, some of it quite dense; its design nevertheless encourages skimming or even just looking at the pictures. *Details*, which seemed an interesting idea at first, now seems to be put together by people who panic at the idea of a reader dwelling on a page for more than a few seconds. The whole theory of the magazine seems to be "Keep 'em moving and they won't notice."

If these were all, say, fashion magazines, this frantic pacing would make more sense. But they are not fashion magazines; they are magazines that treat all life as fashion. Their prose style tends toward anemic irony, arch without being funny, full of in-jokes with neither ins nor jokes. What passes as humor, opinion, or even criticism is largely mass-produced and phony hipsterism.

Being in the know is the mass-producible alternative to being "in society," especially in cities in which what is left of society is reserved for the absurdly rich. Thus the hipster attitudinizing in these magazines both feeds on and encourages reader nervousness: about not belonging, of course, but especially about not getting enough in return for the considerable personal sacrifice one now makes to live in one of our important cities.

In all the yuppiezines, the bulk of the printed matter consists of life-style lecturing, telling us what to buy or eat, where to be and when, what to do when we get there, and even what to think and say, in order to wring the very last wet and delicious drop of satisfaction out of our hard-earned cosmopolitan lifestyles: thus the apotheosis of the restaurant review. No normal person cares about food as much as these reviews imply we all ought to. But the restaurant review is a perfect little nugget of life-style guidance. It packages an entire evening of experience in advance and assures the reader that he will be undertaking an approved activity.

Even *Spy*, which professes to be counter-trendy and offers no consumer advice of the ordinary kind, is devoted mostly to decking out its readers in acceptable opinion (mostly low opinion) and warning them away, by intimidation, from *faux pas*. How many times do we need to be told that Donald Trump is a jerk? *Spy*, in fact, has a particularly low opinion of its readers; it runs on the assumption that they will have no moral objection to the practice of telling quite nasty stories about people for no reason other than casual entertainment.

Though these magazines sell themselves as guidebooks to cosmopolitan culture, they never actually deliver any. No fiction, of course; the magazine fiction market died of other causes. But neither does their criticism or journalism show much creativity or aspire to provide literary entertainment. When their prose is not arch or pretentious, it is terribly bottom-line. It is easy to say that it was ever so, but it simply isn't true. In *The New Yorker* era, critics there and elsewhere clearly wished to delight their readers with good writing, and had a more flattering notion of what would delight them. Just twenty years ago, *New York* spawned the most interesting postwar literary movement, the New Journalism. Today *New York* looks much like any other magazine in the life-style group.

The business of these magazines is not to sell cosmopolitan culture itself, but an illusory affiliation with it. They do not wish their readers to enjoy richer lives, but to be driven to a feeding frenzy by the illusions of life-style. The life-style in question, of course, exists nowhere, and no great number of people could live it if it did. Too few people have the money—and most people are too engaged by the real dramas of their own lives to spend their time frantically pursuing fashionable fun.

Nowhere in these magazines will a reader ever find the suggestion that he or any of his fellows might have a spiritual life, or even a set of principles unconnected to some recent public issue or faddish concern. There have been a few scattered acknowledgments of the Yuppie Return to synagogue or church, but never a serious discussion of the beliefs implied thereby, or whether they might be good or bad, true or not. Certainly religion is not discussed on religion's terms. The Return itself is a fashion story.

These magazines all play to the yuppie myth: the myth of a generation so deeply philistine as to have neither tastes nor principles of its own and thus eager to have all culture reduced to fashion. And this is the portion of the myth one gleans from those publications that cater to the yuppies. In countless conversations today—on politics, real estate values, gentrification, the future of marriage or the family—one quickly discovers that our general image is even worse. The yuppies are hated as much as despised, feared and envied even more often than lampooned: for their supposed success, their individual and collective financial power, and the heartlessness that is assumed to go with these.

The yuppie myth amounts to an accusation of the sort that must remain unstated if it is to remain powerful. For none of us is or ever could be the predatory cartoon character the anti-yuppie brigade denounces. The unstated accusation at the heart of the yuppie myth is this: *Yuppies lack an interior life.*

Say it out loud, and you know it can't be true. We are all blessed or condemned to an inner life. Whether we like it or not, no human being lacks that deeper set of human feelings, desires and aspirations, spiritual and conscientious impulses that feel uniquely personal and yet remain our common heritage, more like than unlike, across the spectrum of humanity. But there is a powerful human impulse to disregard the inner lives of others, to see the rest of humanity as mere objects in a drama of which we are the stars. This impulse is the power pack of all persistent prejudices. It is by denying their share in the common inner life that we make others seem unlike ourselves.

I do not believe the yuppie myth because all the people I know are far more attractively engaged by the realities of life— real loves and real pains, real beliefs and principles, real sacrifices (often on behalf of those principles) and disappointments, real moral and personal dramas, and also real enjoyment of the goods of life and art—than the yuppie myth suggests. Even considered superficially, the myth is untrue. The yuppies proper, the young urban professionals, seem to me remarkable for their education (usually better than that of their parents) and their devotion to the arts and sophisticated entertainment.

But what is there to say to the argument that those who, like the life-style publishers, cater to the yuppie myth prosper precisely because it is true? Does the market lie? Of course it does. The market serves only to allow consumers to choose freely from the items on the menu; it does not ensure that the menu is well designed, or evoke a better menu where there is neither the taste, the imagination, nor the leadership to make one. People must eat. As Jude Wanniski might say, if the market wants duck, and the menu offers only chicken and yak, people will order chicken. That does not prove they like it or are incapable of giving a good duck its due. The debasement of culture in pursuit of yuppie dollars proves only that the myth is powerful, not that it is true.

The so-called yuppies are the most materially, professionally, and politically successful people in the generation now coming to power, a generation already remarkable for the exaggerated influence its sheer size has always given it. Any powerful social myth or prejudice that makes a society's elite seem grossly unattractive to a consensus of the society and even to the elites themselves must be a dangerous and damaging thing. We are the first generation in American history that is despised for trying to establish homes, families, careers, businesses, and identities, that is roundly and regularly condemned for trying to grow up. The ultimate danger of the yuppie myth is that it inspires so much self-hatred, indeed self-denial, in the rising members of my generation. Without an emergency injection of self-esteem, we boomers are not going to be any better at running the country than we have been at inspiring the publishing industry.

In the yuppie myth, we are once again witnessing one of the most powerful recurrent social themes of the last hundred years: the hatred and self-hatred of the bourgeoisie. I am not using the term "bourgeoisie" in its "technical" or Marxist sense: those who own the means of production. Even in Europe in Marx's day, that meaning of the term was never of much use. I mean by the bourgeoisie that now rather large class of people who have the virtues, training, and native abilities that might have enabled them to join Marx's bourgeoisie had they been around in Marx's day, the upper third or so of the middle class; say, amounting in America to some tens of millions of people.

The virtues are the most important part of the deal. The bourgeois virtues are not the highest virtues, but they are those most necessary for success in business and civic affairs: future-directedness, personal discipline, self-reliance, prudence, thrift, diligence, and honesty, or at least square dealing. Add a reasonably good education and a healthy dose of native ability and you'll end up with people who can both provide well for themselves and possess the personal resources to be leaders in civic society. Add a dash of aesthetic refinement and you also get from these people not art and entertainment but a reasonably critical and appreciative audience to support both.

The hatred and self-hatred of this class has long been a major theme of our culture. One of its more powerful expressions, for instance, has been the cult of the artist, which holds that the artist lives on a higher moral and intellectual plane than the bourgeois and is engaged in work that the bourgeois can at best only partly appreciate and certainly cannot criticize. The cult of the artist is a very old idea and it crops up in many cultures. It has been particularly virulent and destructive in this century in America, where it has been the driving force behind much of what is worst in art and literature. In fiction, minimalism certainly was an expression of the cult of the artist, which is why it showed such disregard for the pleasures of the audience. Abstract expressionism was nothing but the cult of the artist, and the pop rebellion against it (which was refreshing even if it didn't yield very good pictures) was aimed mostly at knocking the artist off his pedestal.

Lately, as these examples suggest, the cult has ebbed a bit, and the tide is again running in favor of the audience. Very broadly speaking, postmodernism represents a curbing of artistic arrogance. In yuppie hatred, however, the cult is reborn in a different and dowdier form. What else is the hipster posturing of the life-style magazines for if not to establish a position of superiority for the "artistic" over the bourgeoisie; to enshrine those cosmopolitan few who have the time, money, and inclination to make their lives an expression of fashion; to strike an attitude that will excite in the audience anxiety and envy, and thereby make a sale?

Oh, all right, we're talking about something simple: snobbery. But the forms snobbery takes tell a good deal about a culture. Snobbery has not always taken the form of considering the educated, moderately-to-very-successful literate class to be vapid and pliable philistines. The great strength of *The New Yorker* in its classic period was its firm belief in the equality of the people who read the magazine with those who wrote it. Yes, there was that bit of nonsense about the little old lady from Dubuque, whom they probably underestimated. But on the whole the magazine was driven by its esteem for its audience. Its best reviewers were unpretentious and scrupulously entertaining. They addressed not an audience in need of instruction but a group of friends who shared common tastes. They never doubted that the arts were good insofar as they came up to the standards of the audience. *The New Yorker*'s best essayist was a rather earnest (if entertaining) fellow who believed in the United Nations and whose literary style aimed at brilliance through humility. Did E. B. White ever strike an attitude in order to put the audience in its place? And James Thurber's humor, despite its wonderful cutting edge, was positively homey. If he had ever tried to really *épater* the bourgeoisie, he would have knocked himself on the head. It would be unfair to expect every magazine to be as good as *The New Yorker* was in its best years. But *The New Yorker*, in this particular respect, was typical of its era. We have nothing like it today; whenever the yuppiezines are not sneering at something, they are looking over their shoulders.

We have today a sprinkling of good comic writers and a bumper crop of very talented comedians, but they mostly tend toward Lenny Bruce as watered down by "Saturday Night Live." Their harsh and derisive humor does not so much lampoon bourgeois aspirations as desperately ignore them, as if to recognize the lives that most of their audiences lead, centered on work and family and modest ambitions seriously pursued, would be terminally uncool. When they do lampoon the bourgeoisie, the middle class, their technique is often so extreme as to pass the bounds of satire, which to be well done must always include some sympathy with, or at least comprehension of, the victim. What were the coneheads but a way to lampoon suburban life without having anything to do with it, including thinking about it? In comic films and television, the young bourgeoisie, that is, the yuppies, rarely appear in their bourgeois role. Rather, they are brought onstage dressed for the yuppie Two-Minute Hate as idle or overpaid, incompetent or dishonest, trendy, idiots or creeps.

Comics have always been critics and outsiders. They are not here to run a bourgeoisie support group. But our comics are not outsiders. They are super-insiders. Like rock stars, they are superheroes: idols of subversion, satire, anger, and alienation. They do not criticize what is beneath or outside their notice.

They are still dishing out, and their audience is still lapping up, rock-and-roll comedy, the comedy of adolescent rebellion, not the comedy of people who have to run the country and take care of the kids.

The New Yorker's cartoons are still funny; everyone thinks so. But they could never be squeezed into one of the life-style magazines; they are too sympathetic to what they mock, and they present bourgeois life too accurately. Such realism, such reminders of the true lives of the readers, would completely destroy the atmosphere the life-style magazines seek to create by denying bourgeois life altogether. Contemporary comics are enthusiastically supported by the yuppies. Many of them are very funny. But what does it say about their audience that it so enthusiastically applauds comics who ignore bourgeois life, even as a subject of fun, and whose portrayals of conventionally successful boomers are not only vicious but horribly clichéd? In part, it surely suggests that my generation, far from worshiping material success, is still quite uncomfortable about the qualities that win it for ourselves or others; that rather than growing up rotten, we dislike the idea of having grown up at all.

We are easily intimidated. We are on the defensive, conscious that we are members of the class that dares not speak its name. We lack the self-confidence of our position. We are bourgeois but not phlegmatic, not stout. Although we—as the younger brothers and sisters of the children of the '60s—are quickly making up for lost elegance, it reassures us if we can take that elegance with a bit of punk. The great thing is not to seem pompous, for pomposity has always been the comic Achilles heel of the bourgeoisie. A glance at the fashion ads in those awful magazines makes the point. The models all look either slightly deranged and subversive in a romantic-nihilist sort of way, or ever so arty, or impossibly rich and therefore idle and safe from any stigma of bourgeois orderliness or productivity. Is it fair to say that the models for Calvin Klein's Obsession do not seem like perfect exemplars of the bourgeois virtues?

. . .

The problem with all this is that the bourgeois virtues are essential to a happy, prosperous, well-ordered society. Deprived of those virtues, society will be less happy and people will be less good. The bourgeoisie must be both exemplars and enforcers of those virtues. If the yuppies are taught to hate their class and its virtues, they will do that job much less well, or not at all. Perhaps they will admit defeat, deciding that they really are heartless vulgarians and so to hell with it and everyone. But if they do, then everyone will be the worse for it. The bourgeois life is what nearly everyone in this country actually aspires to; if we punish the achievement of it, it will become almost impossible to achieve.

On the left, the crash of 1987 was regarded in pretty much the same light as AIDS has been in some quarters of the religious right: as an all-too-just punishment from God for the excesses of the yuppie decade. Even the right speaks censoriously of two-earner yuppie families and children abandoned to day care by parents in pursuit of Porsches. This self-satisfied yuppie-bashing, like most self-righteousness, is dangerously self-deluding, an excuse for ignoring a serious problem: young parents today have a far more difficult time than did their parents in achieving a middle-class standard of living, including such basic amenities as decent schools and a safe place for their children to play. Part of the problem is still taxes. Despite Reagan, state, federal, and local governments gouge much more out of us than they took from our parents, enough more to make a real difference in people's standard of living. Yet yuppie-bashing, or what President Bush might call the greed thing, has become an important part of the campaign to make things worse by raising taxes. Anti-greed rhetoric is used profligately by politicians who want more money to spend. The yuppies do a disservice not only to themselves but to the country by not disputing the charge.

But the high price of being middle class goes beyond taxes.

Especially in large cities, which is where the yuppies are, the big price increases result from our getting so much less for those taxes: rotten and dangerous schools, dangerous neighborhoods, crumbling infrastructure. The price of compensating for all these things is terribly high: in wasted (very high) school taxes, in private tuition, in absurd real estate prices that skyrocket as people outbid each other for the last place in a safe neighborhood, or even more extravagantly, a neighborhood with good schools. My neighborhood in Queens has the single great virtue of being crime-free, but no other amenities except for a bit of greenery. It is not conveniently located. But on our block, unstylish fifty-year-old unrenovated two-and-a-half-bedroom row houses sell for a quarter of a million dollars. To buy a home in this modest middle-class neighborhood thus requires a family income of over $75,000. Good public schools do not come in the bargain. My neighbors all pay parochial school tuition. *Of course* the yuppies think too much about money.

Our failure to answer the charges leveled against our generation only confirms the idea that we yuppies are doing just fine, and maybe a bit too well. Unacknowledged and unaddressed, the problems of my generation worsen, not only for the young bourgeoisie, but for the rest of the middle and lower middle class, and for the poor as well. When the bourgeoisie is timid, the whole community suffers. The poor pay the highest price of all for the political impotence of the middle class.

What the bourgeois ideal—well-ordered prosperity in a law-abiding community—needs from the government is only a few basics: good police and fire protection, well-maintained sewers, well-paved streets, safe subways, decent schools. The bourgeoisie does not get much from the expensive exotica of socialism and progressivism: elaborate and often futile interventions into the lives of the poor, government-run housing projects and hospitals and colleges, sex education, AIDS education, and untold dozens of other programs and untold thousands of bureaucrats to administer them. But when yuppie guilt and bourgeois-bashing run high, we become ashamed to insist that getting the basics right is more important than paying for the exotica. To advocate spending less on all those programs directed to the poor and the unusual so we can spend more on the police, who after all are primarily going to arrest the poor and the unusual, is to reveal one's heartless yuppie greed. Yet the poor suffer even more than the middle class from our government's failure to provide the basics our parents took for granted: clean, safe streets and decent schools in orderly neighborhoods.

As I write, the reigning delusion in New York is that the city's number-one problem is racial tension. Yet this city has not had a major racial disturbance for years, despite the very considerable efforts of thugs white and black to start one, and New York has a black mayor even though the electorate is still half white and only a quarter black. Yet no city leader has raised his voice to point out that the best way to curb racial tension would be to double the size of the police force, lift some of the absurd restrictions that keep them from doing their jobs, and curb crime enough to stop white citizens from thinking that the most important thing in life is not to live within mugging distance of black citizens. When the bourgeoisie lacks the confidence to impose on the less successful the same strict standards of behavior it expects from its own members, and lacks the clout to demand that government enforce those standards, then people will be at each other's throats all the time. In the ensuing chaos, the working class, that auxiliary police force of the bourgeoisie, will impose its rough justice on those it (usually wrongly) perceives as enemies of society, which is roughly what happened in Bensonhurst and Howard Beach.

Political power and social influence depend much less on numbers or even money than on confidence and moral authority. I was recently at a large meeting of businessmen and political and economic journalists convened to discuss ways to finance black businesses and rebuild poor black neighborhoods. The keynote speaker was Jesse Jackson. The theme of Jackson's speech, repeated endlessly in his annoying, singsong way, was that we need a great merger of interests between those who "had the means but lacked the moral authority" and those who "had the moral authority but lacked the means," by which he meant the poor, plus of course himself. No one in the room—myself included, I'm sorry to say—stood up and told him to go to hell. I guess he was right about who had the moral authority. Much the same imbalance of power skews art and entertainment: we get rotten efforts from cheap hustlers, testosterone-deficient poseurs, and avaricious cokeheads in part because we lack confidence as an audience and in part because the hustlers, poseurs, and cokeheads have bought the yuppie myth and regard us as their inferiors.

There are stirrings of change. The rather sudden collapse of minimalist fiction certainly was prompted by the younger audiences' enthusiastic reaction to a few new, reasonably serious authors whose best-sellers came equipped with both plots and genuine human concerns. Movies depicting the real lives and concerns of this generation are cropping up more frequently, usually directed by yuppies. The hot, low-budget, highbrow film of the year is Whit Stillman's *Metropolitan*, a witty tribute to the bourgeoisie we have lost. "thirtysomething" at least portrays us as human, if a bit confused, which is about right. Jay Leno, heir apparent to Johnny Carson and one of the most successful comics of our generation, specializes in affectionate teasing of the middle class—his class—and his family, to both of which he is obviously loyal. As for politics, the yuppies remained absolutely invisible in the recent New York City mayoral campaign despite their considerable numbers. But on primary day, the yuppies were the biggest force behind the (losing) candidates associated with such bourgeois interests as public safety. Perhaps we will come out of our shells after all.

Yuppies of the world, unite. You have nothing to lose but that stupid name.

Requiem for the Critical Temper

Roger Kimball

Sharp borderlines everywhere became blurred, and some new, indescribable capacity for entering into hitherto unheard-of relationships threw up new people and new ideas. These people and ideas were not wicked. No, far from it. It was only that the good was adulterated with a little too much of the bad, the truth with error, and the meaning with a little too much of the spirit of accommodation. There positively seemed to be certain proportions in which these elements had to be blended for maximum success in the world. A little admixture of ersatz *was all that was wanted. . . .*

Robert Musil, The Man Without Qualities

I.

For anyone of my generation who began writing criticism in the mid-'80s, it was sometimes difficult not to feel that one was setting out to practice a trade that various cultural developments had rendered obsolete. It was almost as if one had obstinately determined to embark on a career as a blacksmith just as the automobile was supplanting the horse-drawn carriage. The traffic predominating on the cultural thoroughfares was not exactly crying out for one's wares. Of course, there was plenty of writing that called itself criticism. Then as now—though not, alas, so much then as now—the purveyors of public-relations cant and hawkers of politicized academic gibberish dispensed an abundance of material masquerading as criticism.

One needn't have been particularly clever to see that the problems besetting criticism in the early '80s were problems that also affected the arts. Sharp borderlines, as Musil put it, had everywhere become blurred; everywhere there were the hitherto unheard-of relationships, the adulterations, the accommodations. Modernism, the defining artistic force of the twentieth century, had run aground on its own excesses and betrayals. By the '80s, the spirit of aesthetic and existential engagement that had characterized modernism had largely dissipated, veering on the one hand into squamous academic pedantry, on the other into know-nothing radicalism.

In some respects, the new intellectual poverty that had installed itself by the mid-'80s proved even more corrosive than either the pedantry or the radicalism. The horizon of shared knowledge that educated people could once take for granted suddenly collapsed. To be blunt, people didn't know very much. Yes, the newspapers and press releases assured us that we were awash with "culture." More and more people were going to college and graduate school. There were more and more museums, more and more galleries, more and more books, performances, art and non-art events of all kinds. This was the age of the blockbuster—where record crowds paid good money to file past certifiably important works of art—as well as the age in which *everyone* was declared to be an artist. (This widely held sentiment was given a kind of official imprimatur when it was proclaimed by no less an authority than John B. Hightower during his brief tenure as director of the Museum of Modern Art in New York.) But in fact the appetite for serious culture—and *a fortiori* the appetite for serious criticism of culture—was rapidly disappearing.

Not only did this mean that the audience for criticism had

more or less evaporated, it also meant that the young critic found himself in the anomalous situation where criticism was about the last thing that was wanted from critics. Knowledge, clarity, discrimination, insight: increasingly, these traditional critical virtues were regarded as eminently dispensable. Indeed, they somehow acquired an aura of disreputableness. Too much knowledge is a bit boring, you understand, while clarity is a mark of superficiality; one was told that discrimination is fundamentally elitist—and insight: what is it, really, except the codification of prejudice? One regularly heard these and kindred absurdities broadcast by the new "postmodern" guardians of culture. All across the board, in literature, dance, theater, music, and the visual arts, criticism was *out* while politicized cheerleading leavened with a knowing dollop of arcana was *in*.

It is often said that the '60s had opened up new realms of feeling and experience. Today we see that something closer to the opposite is true. In breaking down traditional barriers and assaulting conventional strictures in intellectual, artistic, and moral matters, the boomers did not expand the horizon of human experience but perverted it. Among the many casualties was the independent place granted to art and aesthetic experience. Disinterested criticism is a corollary of that independence, and it, too, was a casualty of the politicization of culture.

In short—despite the odd exception here and there—by the mid-'80s cultural life in this country had become something of a wasteland. It was not, however, a quiet or a somnolent wasteland. As is often the case, the paucity of genuine artistic and intellectual energy was accompanied by spasms of agitation and clamoring for attention. For one thing, there was a nearly ubiquitous pose of originality, of daring, of being on the cutting edge, as artists and then critics competed with each other to be more and more outrageous. Behind the pretentious gestures and the hype, what one mostly saw was a handful of debased modernist clichés updated and recycled *ad nauseam*. The inanities of "performance art," which really got going around this time, and the rebarbative "deconstructivist" nonsense that managed to get passed off as criticism are among the main legacies this period has bequeathed us.

II.

Now, as we enter the '90s, it is clear that cultural life in this country is dominated on one side by the politicized obscurities oozing out of the academy, on the other side by the vacuous maunderings of a media-addicted art establishment. The effect this has had on the general cultural climate has been divisive and cheapening; the effect it has had on the practice of criticism has been disastrous.

In the academy we have seen the institutionalization of a whole range of radical absurdities. College curricula—like college faculty appointments—are increasingly being determined by radical political imperatives. In the name of scholarship, university presses are disgorging mountains of politicized tripe that is as unintelligible as it is noxious. In one of a series of new courses replacing the previous requirement in Western culture at Stanford University, freshmen watch movies, read the writings of the Algerian revolutionary Frantz Fanon, and attend classes with inspiring titles like "Our Bodies, Our Sheep, Our Cosmos, Ourselves."

Other examples abound. At its 1989 meeting, the prestigious Modern Language Association countenanced all manner of dubious investigations, including a symposium called "The Muse of Masturbation" at which one could learn all about "Jane Austen and the Masturbating Girl." And then there is the extent to which popular culture has invaded the academy, replacing traditional objects of study and providing new grist for the mills of pedantry. The combination of popular culture and French-inspired critical theory has proved to be especially lethal. For example, in an unbearably pretentious study of rock-and-roll music videos by E. Ann Kaplan, a professor of English and director of the humanities center at the State University of New York at Stony Brook, we read that "the plethora of gender positions on [MTV] is arguably linked to the heterogeneity of current sex roles and to an imaginary [sic] constructed out of a world in which all traditional categories, boundaries, and institutions are being questioned. . . . The romantic video," Professor Kaplan concludes, "functions in the pre-symbolic dyadic terrain between the illusory merging with the mother and the phallicism that follows the mirror phase." Got that?

It has been clear for some time that such developments represent an intellectual and moral debacle for the academy.* Perhaps less obvious is the way in which the academicization of cultural life has been a debacle for the general practice of criticism. Ironically, the triumph of the academy, far from elevating the intellectual level of critical discourse, has coarsened it immeasurably. Because the academy is the largest and most powerful arbiter of intellectual fashion in our culture, the standards of taste and value it sanctions exert an enormous pressure on culture as a whole. The appropriation, and the abuse, of the critical spirit by the academy has seduced many baby boom critics into espousing the politicized cant regnant in the academy; unable to envision an alternative, these writers simply mouth the catchphrases they absorbed in the classroom. The idea of independent critical judgment is dismissed as a perfidious ideological construct even as clarity of expression has been rendered suspect through desuetude.

This is not to say that evidence of decay is confined to the academy and its satellites. Such decay is patent in all our most important cultural institutions. One thinks, for example, of the unfortunate habit adopted by many museums of supplying—for a charge, of course—tape-recorded "tours" of their most popular exhibitions. The taped commentary is generally narrated by a

---

* My book *Tenured Radicals: How Politics Has Corrupted Our Higher Education* (Harper & Row) provides a chronicle of this debacle.

curator or the director of the museum, though sometimes a show-business celebrity is called upon to do the honors. These seemingly innocuous productions are immensely popular with the throngs that slog through the exhibitions; nevertheless, they commit a fraud on anyone interested in experiencing art first-hand. Instead of encouraging people to *look* at the works of art before their eyes, they have the effect of transforming them into mere illustrations of the commentary droning on over the headsets. Armed with their taped primers, the visitors are well equipped to sail through any exhibition unscathed by a direct encounter with the art they supposedly came (and in many cases paid) to see.

The proliferation of these tape-recorded commentaries is a sterling illustration of the principle that things are always worse than one had thought. No sooner had one gotten used to the spectacle of glassy-eyed crowds moving through galleries at a pace dictated by the murmuring voice buzzing in their ears than something quite incredible happened. The headsets and tape recorders began appearing at the *press previews* of exhibitions as well. The sociology of the museum press preview—what is now often, and more accurately, referred to as the "media preview" —is itself a subject worthy of detailed examination. These events have become so crowded in recent years that, if one didn't know better, one might think that the number of critics seriously interested in the arts has suddenly mushroomed.

But, alas, one does know better. It has been obvious for some time that a good deal of the "criticism" that appears in our magazines and newspapers is little more than an elaborated précis of a press release distributed beforehand by the museum. Yet apparently even that process was too demanding or too chancy. For now many members of "the press" flit blithely through an exhibition with headset firmly in place, forming their opinions in the most painless way possible: ingesting them wholesale from someone else.

What else can one do if one doesn't know anything? Among the most blatant—and also most pathetic—illustrations I have witnessed of the current crisis in criticism came during the press preview for the great exhibition of Monet's series paintings from the 1890s that opened at the Museum of Fine Arts in Boston in the winter of 1990. I was about halfway through the exhibition when a "critic" for a major American newspaper came up to my companion, enthused for a moment about the paintings, and then cheerfully admitted that they all seemed so much alike to him that it was impossible for him to distinguish the better ones from the worse. In other words, he blithely admitted that he hadn't a clue about how to evaluate them critically.

The character of the contemporary critical climate also shows itself in the fate of certain exemplary reputations. For instance, the extraordinary extent to which T. S. Eliot's once unassailable reputation has plummeted in recent years says a great deal about what our contemporary critics and cultural tastemakers value—or, rather, what they no longer value. Similarly, when one considers the hogwash that is bruited about as important criticism today, the quiet but seemingly inexorable eclipse of W. H. Auden's once-towering presence on the cultural scene speaks volumes. It was revealing, for example, to learn that Auden's collected works were to be published not by Random House, the large commercial house that had published his work in this country for decades, but by Princeton University Press. Even ten years ago it would have been inconceivable that a publisher would willingly relinquish so important and so vital an author as Auden. But clearly even Auden has come to seem less important and less vital—has in fact become something of a specialized, recondite interest. When Princeton brought out the first volume of his works in 1989, the publication party, held at a small bookstore in Greenwich Village, was a lackluster affair that drew only about twenty people. Again, even ten years ago, one could not have imagined the first volume of Auden's collected works being published without a huge fanfare and celebration. Today, such literary fetes are reserved for the likes of E. L. Doctorow and Norman Mailer.

III.

In attempting to understand the fate of criticism today and its prospects for the '90s, it may be useful to look back to a time when the climate for criticism was more hospitable. Consider the year 1950—hardly ancient history, but safely before any of the contributors to this volume were born. Politically, 1950 meant the Cold War, Joseph McCarthy, the Alger Hiss case. It was a time when old-guard Marxist rhetoric still shouted from the pages of the left-wing press.

From the perspective of the '90s, 1950 also seems to us to have been a time of cultural giants: of Eliot, Auden, Pound, Stevens; Picasso, Giacometti, Matisse; Sartre, Heidegger, Wittgenstein, Arendt; Balanchine and Stravinsky. Where are the writers, thinkers, and artists of such stature today? They do not exist. Nor is it clear that, if they did exist, such individuals could assume the defining cultural role they once had. The audience for Philip Glass is not Stravinsky's audience any more than the devotees of Andy Warhol or Cindy Sherman can be said to be admirers of Picasso or Matisse. Our vaunted cultural "pluralism" is really a destructive cultural promiscuity. It may be heresy to say so, but, in the deepest sense, a taste for the cynical frivolousness of a Warhol or a Sherman renders one incapable of appreciating great art.

The cultural character of an age is to a large extent defined by individual geniuses. But it is sustained and directed by the caliber of critical exchange it inspires, not only among critics and artists, but also—to employ a phrase that seems increasingly anachronistic—among the educated public that cares about art and culture. One important indication of a generation's critical temper is to be found in its journals and periodicals. It is there that one can witness the life of ideas unfolding—or failing to unfold, as the case may be—in discussion and debate.

Thus was the critical temper of the early '50s evident in the reception accorded to Lionel Trilling's landmark collection of critical essays, *The Liberal Imagination: Essays on Literature and Society*, which appeared in 1950. Trilling's book is perhaps best seen as a liberal attack on the spiritual limitations of liberalism. It is a measure of how drastically things have changed in our culture, however, that what was intended as a liberal critique of liberalism should now appear as a defense of conservative values. Beginning with the assertion that "nowadays there are no conservative or reactionary ideas in general circulation," Trilling went on to warn that this was an unhealthy state of affairs because "it is not conducive to the real strength of liberalism that it should occupy the intellectual field alone." Trilling's effort to expose the emotional shallowness of liberalism concentrated on the way various manifestations of the liberal imagination pervert humane values. The great internal threat to liberalism was simplification: the tendency to reduce or flatten out experience, limit possibility, curtail the imagination. But it is important to remember that Trilling's purpose was as much moral as intellectual. The sense of "variousness and possibility" he hoped to encourage through the critical study of literature was directed not simply at the enlargement of experience but at the humanization and refinement of experience. Thus at the end of his scathing review of the Kinsey Report on sexuality, he writes that "although it is possible to say of the Report that it brings light, it is necessary to say of it that it spreads confusion." Heralded as a liberating revelation of the "variousness" of human sexuality, the Kinsey Report in fact represented, as Trilling saw, the dehumanization of sexuality and hence the impoverishment of experience.

The enormous attention—and the *quality* of the attention—that Trilling's book occasioned in the literary journals of the time is something one can scarcely imagine today. One thinks, for example, of R. P. Blackmur's essay on the book for *The Kenyon*

Review. The piece is nothing if not admiring; but it nonetheless begins with the sobering observation that as a critic Trilling "cultivates a mind never entirely his own." Anyone familiar with *The Liberal Imagination* will recognize that with this two-edged formulation Blackmur has summarized an important source of both Trilling's strengths and his weaknesses as a critic—namely, his often unmodulated reliance on borrowed theoretical machinery.

Blackmur also recognized that behind the diversity of subjects Trilling discussed in *The Liberal Imagination* there was a powerful unifying concern. "Mr. Trilling requires the development, not the attrition of values in the conflict between morals and experience," Blackmur explained; "and his chief complaint is against the attrition of value after value, often mistaken for hardening, and sometimes for the prophecy, of value in the contemporary American mind." Blackmur's phrase "the attrition of values" not only sums up the main obsession of *The Liberal Imagination*—the fate of what Trilling calls the "moral imagination"—it also signals the unabashedly serious nature of his generation's commitment to the vocation of criticism. "If you see your great subject as the politics of human power," Blackmur continued,

> and are confronted by a world which sees its subject as power simply, a world which is fearful of politics and distrustful of the human, you have your maximum right to moral indignation. And if you see your colleagues in the liberal imagination going along with that world, you will say . . . that the loss amounts to the loss of the prevailing sense of human politics, the loss of piety, of history, and purpose.

"Piety," "history," "purpose": their loss is real, even if we hardly understand what such words mean anymore.

As one looks back at the year 1950, three journals in particular stand out as arenas where criticism flourished: *The Nation*, which had been founded in 1865, *Partisan Review*, which had been founded in 1934, and *The Hudson Review*, a relative new-comer which had been on the scene only since 1947. Flipping through their pages, one is struck by many things. In *The Nation*, at any rate, a sometimes virulent leftism is on display; one dis-covers even such latter-day cold warriors as Reinhold Niebuhr blathering about "the embattled American plutocracy, finding political power slipping from its hands," etcetera. But what is surprising is not the left-wing politics bedecking the front pages but—especially as one considers *The Nation* in its current incar-nation—the suspension of overt political imperatives in its cul-tural sections, in which one could still find a good deal of sober critical writing.

Then there are those little *frissons* that the passage of years engenders. Thus we read in the September/October issue of *Par-tisan Review* in 1950 that "Bernard Malamud is a young writer who lives in Oregon. 'The First Seven Years' is one of his first published stories." Anyone of my generation knows that it is quite out of the question that Bernard Malamud should have *ever* been a young writer publishing his first story. (These days, it is also hard to credit Delmore Schwartz's observation, in a review of short stories, that "*The New Yorker* obviously has no political views." Tell *that* to "The Talk of the Town.")

Of course, looking back through the issues of these journals that appeared in 1950, one is also is struck by the parade of names. In *Partisan Review*, one had Ernst Robert Curtius on Ortega y Gasset, Clement Greenberg on art, a symposium on religion and the intellectuals whose participants included A. J. Ayer, R. P. Blackmur, and Sidney Hook; there were pieces by W. H. Auden, Raymond Aron, Saul Bellow, Hannah Arendt, and on and on. In *The Hudson Review* that year, one found work by Ezra Pound, Joseph Kerman, W. H. Auden, T. S. Eliot; in *The Nation*, one found Lionel Trilling, Diana Trilling, Randall Jarrell, and others of similar stature.

Even more impressive than the grand figures that present themselves one after the next in these volumes is the general level of critical discourse, civility, and the respect for clarity of expression. In the matter of civility, at least, *The Hudson Review*—perhaps because it was not in thrall to any identifiable political agenda—is the most notable. There is, for example, a marvelous discussion of verse drama by the journal's editor, Frederick Morgan, on the occasion of the New York performance of Eliot's *The Cocktail Party*. One can scarcely imagine such a piece appearing today—partly because there are no Eliots writing good verse drama, but partly because there is so little interest in serious criticism of this kind.

In that same issue there is also another intelligent review of *The Liberal Imagination*, this one by the well-known scholar R. W. B. Lewis—I wonder if he has done anything so impressive since—as well as an amusing dialogue with W. H. Auden. About psychiatrists, who were a more prominent fixture in cultural life then than now, Auden correctly observed that "some of them are power-maniacs. About half of them are quacks. They think they have all the answers. I would much rather have the police in charge than psychiatrists. The police can always be bribed."

One's first reaction to so much good work is exhilaration. Exhilaration is followed quickly by melancholy, however, for it is clear that, whatever virtues these or other journals abroad today possess, the critical climate of the age has decayed drastically. In his classic 1923 essay "The Function of Criticism," T. S. Eliot described the critic's task with unsurpassed simplicity and accuracy. "Roughly speaking," Eliot wrote, the aim of criticism is "the elucidation of works of art and the correction of taste."

Like many of Eliot's essays from this period, "The Function of Criticism" had an enormous influence. The mandarin authority of the prose, the fluent, cosmopolitan learning, the self-confident exercise of literary discrimination at the highest level: these were among the qualities that made him the most important and widely emulated literary critic of the century. Writing in *The Nation* in 1950, the art critic Clement Greenberg—himself a towering figure in the ranks of twentieth-century criticism and not someone given to dispensing idle praise—described Eliot as "the greatest of all literary critics." But think of how Eliot's description of the critic's task would sound today. Let us leave aside the question of what Eliot would count as a genuine work of art. (Imagine: T. S. Eliot on Joan Didion.) Consider only his demand that critics seek to provide elucidation and the correction of taste. Elucidation? Correction? Taste? Already these were strange words when I began writing criticism in 1983. Today they are on their way to being placed on our new Multicultural Index of Forbidden Terms.

At a moment when, as Robert Musil foresaw, something *ersatz* is added to almost everything in the cultural world, Eliot's words provide us not only with a measure of what we have lost, but also a model for what we might regain. Despite the declared triumph of various "postmodernisms," there has been no convincing successor to the spirit of modernism in our culture. At the center of the modernist ethos is a seriousness about art and culture that invests the critical enterprise with a responsibility that is as much moral as it is aesthetic. The arts matter because they tell us something important about the central aspirations and failures of the human spirit; criticism matters because it tells us something important about the aspirations and failures of art.

It is thus hardly surprising that there has always been a prominent religious element in modernism. Even where it is atheistic—even where it is specifically hostile to religion—modernism attempts to pose the deepest questions in the most sustained way possible. For the modernist, culture is a spiritual endeavor. Thumbing through the critical writings of a Cleanth Brooks, a T. S. Eliot, a Clement Greenberg, an R. P. Blackmur, one is impressed not only by the intellectual range these writers commanded but also by their earnestness. Perhaps we do not particularly notice the absence of these things today. But might it not be that, as Blackmur put it in his review of *The Liberal Imagination*, "the loss is unnoticed because it is total"?

How to Succeed in the Lit Biz Without Really Trying

Donna Rifkind

*E*very so often, the urge to revive the "generation roundup"—the presumption that people of a specific age can be said to sum themselves up with a single common characteristic—gets dusted off and pressed into service. Now that the century's end is truly in sight and the first signs of millenarianism are starting to surface, the generation roundup begins to seem, I suppose, even more tempting; here is a chance to assess the *fin de siècle* from the point of view of the ostensibly homogeneous group now coming of age.

I don't really believe in the generation roundup. Common sense would suggest that there were lots of good talkers in the Silent Generation and that plenty of people of the Lost Generation found their way without too many problems. The generation roundup's usefulness, which seems to me dubious at best, becomes even more problematic in its current incarnation, the "baby boom generation." For here is a group that appears to be defined solely by the fact that there are a lot of people who belong to it.

My subject is literary careerism among the baby boomers, but it strikes me that writers coming of age today do not behave in ways that are all that different from writers of previous generations. What *has* changed—though only by becoming more overheated—is the so-called publishing world, the environment in which writers write and by which their success is measured.

The word "careerism," of course, contains an implied judgment: the dictionary defines it as "the policy or practice of advancing one's career, often at the cost of one's integrity." I don't wish to give the impression that I believe all writers are guilty of giving up their integrity; that would be as reductive as claiming that all people of a specific generation tend to behave in the same way. But young writers who are just beginning to think about what their profession demands of them are often misled right out of the starting gate. All too often, creative-writing courses, writers' workshops, and the literary establishment as a whole put too much emphasis on the importance of planning career strategies and not enough on the writer's devotion to his craft and the maintenance of his artistic integrity. And this neglect of integrity is an unquestionably bad thing to encourage in people whose business is the art of persuasion.

1. *How to Write a Book That Will Last Ten Years*

So much has been written about the glamorous lives of certain young baby boom writers that another discussion of the subject would be unlikely to inspire anything but a lot of yawns and teeth-gnashing. But, as I mentioned, I want to discuss contemporary literary life in a more general way, a way that recognizes careerism in the American publishing world as an old phenomenon that's new again. The pertinent questions for every aspiring young writer now coming out of the workshops and graduate school programs, for every lawyer or stockbroker with hopes for an unfinished novel in the drawer, are these: What is literary success? How is success measured in today's writing market? Is it possible to escape the kind of flash-in-the-pan celebrity that threatens to ruin nearly every newly published young author? *Is there such a thing any more as literary longevity?*

In 1938, the editor and writer Cyril Connolly published a book called *Enemies of Promise* in which he posed what he considered to be the greatest challenge to authors: that of writing a book that will last ten years. (Never mind the dream of one's work lasting through eternity—ten years, even in the late '30s, when Hemingway and Joyce were in their prime, would do.) "Contemporary books do not keep," Connolly warned. "The quality in them which makes for their success is the first to go; they turn overnight." He went on:

> What kills a literary reputation is inflation. The advertising, publicity and enthusiasm which a book generates—in a word its success—imply a reaction against it. The element of inflation in a writer's success, the extent to which it has been forced, is something that has to be written off. One can fool the public about a book but the public will store up resentment in proportion to its folly. The public can be fooled deliberately by advertising and publicity or it can be fooled by accident, by the writer fooling himself.

It is interesting to observe that among the books Connolly cited as examples of this fraudulence were Evelyn Waugh's *Decline and Fall* and Aldous Huxley's *Brave New World*. Neither novel is a masterpiece, but few critics these days would consider them with anywhere near as much contempt as Connolly did. Not to mention that they both far outlasted Connolly's ten-year limit, and are in fact almost certainly read more frequently today than *Enemies of Promise*.

Connolly's dour reflections on the perishability of literary reputation, written more than forty years ago, remind us that what's happening today in the world of publishing has been going on in much the same way for decades. It would be short-sighted indeed to suppose that a tongue-lashing like the one that novelist Jay McInerney delivered to a number of literary critics in the July 1989 issue of *Esquire* signals anything like a new phenomenon. Entitled "The Writers of Wrong: A Novelist Carves the Critics," McInerney's article attempted to show that critics today are more interested in "youth-bashing," in destroying young writers' reputations, than in encouraging them.

McInerney's piece had all the foot-stomping, curse-slinging charm of a teenager in a tantrum. He went to great lengths to defend his beleaguered young colleagues Bret Easton Ellis and Tama Janowitz, whose first novels were "whacked sadistically," "thrash[ed] mercilessly," and "trashed" by critics. "As any novice book reviewer knows," McInerney explained, "a puff piece gets the novelist's name out there while a hatchet job gets *your* name in circulation. If as a critic you wish to generate a little . . . self-*hype*, well. . . ." Poor Ellis and Janowitz, mourned McInerney, forced to languish in obscurity while the mean old critics got all the attention. Never mind that both young authors received sums for movie deals that could not have totaled less than five zeros, or that Janowitz's book suffered so much neglect that it inspired the installment of a "Slaves of New York" boutique at Bloomingdale's.

McInerney's screed went on in the same semihysterical vein for some time, triumphantly rescuing other heroic young literary figures from the jowls of the evil reviewers. But there were few readers at the time who believed that McInerney was as genuinely altruistic toward his fellow writers as he was pretending to be. Though he mentioned his own fiction only tangentially in the piece, it was fairly obvious from the level of his fury that his attack was fueled by a great deal of self-interest, and that he conceived the piece at least partially in response to the sour reviews for his own second and third novels, *Ransom* and *Story of My Life*, which followed the tremendous success—both critical and financial—of his first book, *Bright Lights, Big City*.

What happened to McInerney was precisely what Connolly was talking about in the passage I quoted above: he gained his initial triumph by publishing a novel of some talent but by no means a work of genius; his later efforts proved to be less good than the first; critics, perhaps feeling cheated by the lack of return on the author's early promise, regretted the stupendous amount of hype they had lavished on the first novel and vented their fury through overly splenetic negative reviews. McInerney's counterattack, reeking as it did of inexperience and poor sportsmanship, was nevertheless somewhat understandable in the circumstances. Had *Bright Lights* not received such inflated attention at the beginning, the reviewers' ferocity and McInerney's ensuing bad feelings—all equally inflated—might have been avoided. This is not to suggest that *Ransom* or *Story of My Life* would have secured a place among the best books of the century if the publicity machine had been turned down a notch. But perhaps McInerney would have concentrated less on the highly publicized idle pleasures his success brought him and more on developing his talent as a writer.

I mention Jay McInerney not in order to present new evidence about him as an author—almost everybody would agree that too much attention, both positive and negative, has been paid him already—but to show him to be a representative victim of the celebrity mill that seems to control today's publishing world. McInerney is a victim of a quite different kind, however, from the ones he described in his *Esquire* article; the current publishing world is a much more complex, impersonal environment than one which consists only of nice, neat Oedipal relationships between young authors and older critics. It's a world where the balance is all wrong: the emphasis is on quick success, not achievement; on trying to stay in the spotlight for fifteen minutes, not on trying to write a book that will last ten years. Again, there is nothing terribly new about this, except for the increasing speed with which new authors emerge and disappear.

As everyone is aware, the intimate, leisurely days of publishing have long been over; taking their cue from television and the movies, publishing's bywords are "fast track," "high concept," "corporate merger," and "marketability." More books are published these days than ever before. During 1987–88, 90,000 new book titles were listed in *Books in Print*, as compared with 8,000 in 1949–50. At the same time, 50,000 to 60,000 titles are declared out of print annually. This means, of course, that most books published today have a very short shelf life, causing the pace of American publishing to seem faster every day.

Within this environment, writers might easily feel forced to shape themselves into recognized public figures as quickly as possible, by whatever means they can invent, so as not to be pushed out of the race. Where do young authors today get their ideas for planning careers as media stars? Gerald Howard, an editor for the publishing house of W. W. Norton, offered an explanation for how the contemporary publishing world contributes to the writer's longings for fame in an article in *The American Scholar* for Summer 1989. In the piece, entitled "Mistah Perkins —He Dead: Publishing Today," Howard talked about the understandable yearning serious writers feel for the huge sums of money that inferior writers earn for best-selling hack jobs—huge even after last year's publishing slump and subsequent cutbacks —and the "disproportionate praise and attention (and money) lavished on the upstart of the moment."

> Little wonder [Howard continued] that some of these writers decide that writing well is insufficient revenge, that a system so manifestly incapable of matching reward to merit deserves to be subverted and manipulated. I believe that a number of important American writers have made some such conscious internal decision to maneuver cold-bloodedly for the big time, and I cannot say that I blame them. Their publishers are most likely parts of huge corporations, they've probably had too many editors in their careers to depend on

them very much, the faith that art can save your soul is a quaint and dying creed, the surrounding literary culture is thin and fragmented and unsustaining— why subsist on such thin gruel as a prestigious literary career?

Who, moreover, can blame young authors for taking stock of this situation and reaching similarly cynical conclusions about how they should proceed?

2. How to Create an Image That Lasts Fifteen Minutes

I want to back up a minute here, to the time before a young author's first novel hits the presses. Let's say he (or she) has enrolled in a writer's workshop such as the one at the University of Iowa. There, with the advice and encouragement of his teacher, an established author with a Big Name, he will have written his first book-length manuscript—most likely a novel or a book of short stories, but possibly a volume of essays or poetry. The Big Name will show it to his own publisher, who agrees to publish the work. All indications would point to the fact that this young author is well on his way.

But I would object that this young author's career is already in serious trouble, even before his first book is published. For in the time that passes between the sale of his novel and a year or two after its publication, he will no doubt have spent much less time formulating and writing a new project than planning strategies that will enable him to capitalize on his initial success. That is, he will go to readings and publication parties. He will make "important contacts" with other writers. He will "network." He will have lunch with publishers and agents. None of these, of course, are evil or deplorable activities; they are fun, after all, and a just reward for the young author's previous hard work. But the fact is that, while the young author has undoubtedly created a full-time career for himself, it is a career that has nothing at all to do with the career of literature.

These activities could very well signal the end of the line for this author as a producer of potentially valuable literary work. Such is the structure of the publishing world that an author's youth, which almost everyone considers an asset, is actually a liability. For the inexperience and malleability that go along with youth almost always tend to steer authors like this one to the path of least resistance: to the path, that is, where all the spotlights are hung, the path where one goes hoping to stay bathed in the warmth and praise that initially felt so good. Given the amount of encouragement from everyone around him, a young author can hardly be faulted for choosing this particular path. It seems so clearly to be the correct one.

Cyril Connolly presented the situation with characteristic acuity when he wrote, again in *Enemies of Promise,*

> A young writer must be careful not to pay the world more attention than it gives him, he may satirise it but is not advised to celebrate it, nor become its champion, for the moribund will turn on their defenders. . . . Success is a kind of moving staircase, from which an artist, once on, has great difficulty in getting off, for whether he goes on writing well or not, he is carried upwards, encouraged by publicity, by fan-mail, by the tributes of critics and publishers and by the friendly clubmanship of his new companions.

But Connolly didn't have any especially satisfactory suggestions for avoiding these pitfalls. At times, in fact, he could be downright vicious, offering such drippingly ironic advice for literary success as: "The health of a writer should not be too good, and perfect only in those periods of convalescence when he is not writing." He was at his least charitable in his famous, chilling advice to the effect that the best writers ought to have no personal family lives at all, that "there is no more sombre enemy of good art than the pram in the hall."

I would be surprised to learn that anybody ever actually took Connolly's suggestions to heart, especially after they figured out that his bitterness toward other writers was caused in part by his own failure to produce a literary masterpiece. (In 1944, Connolly made a statement that contains perhaps more contempt and despair than he intended: "The more books we read," he wrote, "the clearer it becomes that the true function of a writer is to produce a masterpiece and that no other task is of any consequence.")

The more you examine it, the more you discover that *Enemies of Promise* is actually a very strange little book, a literary curiosity with a certain pointed effectiveness, but one that cannot be taken altogether seriously. It is useful because it offers an exact formulation of the perils that success holds for writers, both in Connolly's time and in our own. It does not, however, offer any solutions at all.

3. Careerism vs. Vocation

People who write for a living almost always say that they knew they wanted to be a writer from the time they were children. Writing is, to use a couple of very outdated words, a vocation or calling, something you do because long ago something or someone—a disembodied voice, some people say—instructed you to do it. The word "vocation," of course, once meant a religious calling, and indeed there is something almost religious about the vocation of literature: you can't really explain your devotion to it, but you don't question it, either.

Can a writer remain faithful to his calling and still profit from all the rewards of what the contemporary publishing world considers a successful career? I think so, depending on the writer. But I also think that in most cases the sacredness of the calling becomes debased by the writer's complacent image of himself as a so-called success. I offer as an example a comment the novelist Mona Simpson made in a 1987 *New York Times* article, much remarked upon at the time of its publication, called "New York's Spinning Literary Circles." Simpson was talking about going to a reading given by a favorite writer (presumably a Big Name) and running into other young writers. "You catch up with people you haven't seen in a year," Simpson said, "so someone will have had a baby, or moved into a new apartment. You don't see the texture as much. But everyone in the room will have read Proust."

Simpson clearly felt a warm, safe sense of community in the gathering she described in this statement. But is this why writers have all struggled to read Proust, or *Lost Illusions,* or *War and Peace?* So they can meet at gatherings that have all the literary intensity of a high school reunion and check up on babies and new apartments? I was under the impression that the reason people devote themselves to writing is that literature of even the most realistic kind transforms these trivialities, elevates them to a higher plane. Simpson's comment, with its inherent snobbishness and self-congratulation—she clearly finds worthwhile only the company of people who have read Proust—has absolutely nothing at all to do with the vocation of literature.

The vocation of literature has no place for snobbishness—it has no place, in truth, for cliques or communities of any kind, literary or otherwise. Diversions notwithstanding, the vocation of literature is a purely lonely enterprise. It doesn't offer any of the communal rewards one conventionally associates with writers—no kind words from the publishing establishment or from one's peers, no encouraging advice, no self-indulgent diatribes in national magazines against your critics, not even a friendly lunch. It offers only one reward, one that for many people is not anywhere near enough to keep them going. The reward—trite, unspectacular, unhip as it sounds—is the sheer exhilaration of the process of creating a work of art.

4. Eyes on the Prize

Does this mean that writers should completely ignore any recognition that comes their way? There have been many conflicting
opinions; along with Connolly, Robert Louis Stevenson thought
the answer to this question ought to be yes. In a "Letter to a
Young Gentleman Who Proposes to Embrace the Career of Art,"
Stevenson wrote: "There should be no honours for the artist . . .
he has already, in the practice of his art, more than his share of
the rewards of life; the honours are pre-empted for other trades,
less agreeable and perhaps more useful." Joseph Epstein, in his
book *Plausible Prejudices*, concurred, claiming, "The only prize
serious writers can unequivocally esteem is good readers."

Epstein reached this conclusion after commenting on the
fact that these days there seem to be more literary prizes to
bestow every year than there are writers to claim them, so that
the value of these prizes is beginning to seem more and more
inflated. I have to acknowledge the truth of this phenomenon,
but I'm not in complete agreement that literary prizes—that is,
rewards and recognitions in all their current manifestations, from
offers for movie deals to fan letters—ought to be avoided altogether. Certainly no one I know, myself included, would be so
ludicrously high-minded as to turn down a writing prize. The
question seems to me to be less an either/or problem than one of
balance, of proportion. Edward Gibbon, writing about literary
persistence, once claimed that he wrote with the objective of
gaining "some fame, some profit, and the assurance of daily
amusement." In my view, as long as the third element in Gibbon's formulation—and by "daily amusement" I understand
Gibbon to mean not only amusement but the deeper pleasure of
spiritual or intellectual discovery and growth—is not thrown
completely away, fame and profit (in moderation, and with the
recognition of their fleeting value) do not necessarily spell disaster for a literary career.

Henry James, while offering advice once to young novelists, recommended that they should "be generous and delicate and pursue the prize." As James's biographer Leon Edel interprets this, "The prize for him had always been the treasure of his craft. He felt powerful because he knew that his imagination could transfigure life." That power James felt was the elusive power Connolly was searching for, the power that could make a book last ten years and more. It's a power that, achieved after years of lonely pursuit, must surely be worth more than some ephemeral publicity for insufficient effort.

I am sure that there are young writers today, even among those who have already had a book published, who are concentrating more on the "treasure of their craft" than on persuading Toni Morrison or Larry McMurtry to write a blurb for their next book, or on bad-mouthing critics for writing harsh reviews. And I'm equally sure that it will be these writers who, rather than concentrating on creating a name for themselves, will be creating the most valuable literature of our time. What I'm talking about is a truth so utterly commonplace that a lot of people have been lured into forgetting it: careerism is a poor choice for a writer to make, however rich its superficial rewards may seem.

In her book *Art and Ardor*, Cynthia Ozick recalls a similar lesson she learned as a young writer from Henry James. In "The Lesson of the Master," she writes:

The true Lesson of the Master, then, is simply, never to venerate what is complete, burnished, whole, in its grand organic flowering or finish—never to look toward the admirable and dazzling end; never to be ravished by the goal; never to worship ripe Art or the ripened artist; but instead to seek to be young while young, primitive while primitive, ungainly when ungainly—to look for crudeness and rudeness, to husband one's own stupidity or ungenius.

For our diverse, energetic generation of writers, I would like to see stupidity used this wisely. I would like to see all that energy put to better use than the garnering of publicity and fan mail. I would like to see an end to young writers' premature complacence about their far from perfect achievements, however promising those achievements may be. And I would hope that for myself, though I am only a book reviewer—a low-ranking member of the literary establishment, the kind that real writers like Jay McInerney hate—I will be able to look back one day and see that I have followed my own unsensational, old-fashioned, and rather obvious advice.

Everything You Know Is Wrong

Andrew Ferguson

*I*n 1974—it could have been 1975, maybe 1973—the Firesign
Theater, a once-celebrated drugs-and-surrealism comedy troupe
of the '60s, released a splendid record album. The record pur-
ported to be a radio broadcast by a seer named Dr. Happy Harry
Cox, who lived in a nudist trailer park in Hellmouth, California.
Dr. Cox was the possessor of much secret knowledge. "Did you
know," he asked his listeners, "that everything you know is
wrong?" His revelations were startling. Dogs fly spaceships. The
Aztecs invented the vacation. A giant sun burns at the center of
the earth. Men and women are the same sex. The South won the
Civil War. And so on.

The more I think about it these fourteen or fifteen or thirteen years later, the more I'm convinced that the Firesign Theater was on to something. Two experiences in particular have
lately caused me to reexamine the Happy Harry thesis. Not long
ago, I was wandering around the Iwo Jima memorial, across the
river from Washington, trying to decide whether that famous
momument's socialist-realist dimensions were really a proper
rendering of the extraordinary men who captured the first slice
of Japanese territory in World War II. I found myself next to a
pair of young men about my age. One turned to the other and
said, "You know this was faked."

"Yeah?" said his friend.

"It was P.R.," said the first man. "They had to fake the whole thing. One guy really put the flag up there. Then, like a week later, the general got a cameraman and he made these guys go up there with a much bigger, flashier flag. They practiced putting the flag up for hours. There were no Japs around. These guys had to do it a bunch of times before they got it right. The whole thing was just for propaganda reasons. And they released the picture to make it look spontaneous. Like it was this big dangerous thing."

"Yeah?" his friend said again. The first fellow looked deeply serious and, to tell the truth, a shade self-congratulatory—as if he had caught a chronic liar in an embarrassing whopper.

A couple of months later I visited Canterbury, Kent, and was up early one day for my morning constitutional. Down a winding side street, not a hundred yards from the cathedral where Saint Thomas Becket met his unhappy fate at the hands of Henry II's courtiers, I glanced in the window of a bookseller and saw a piece of curled parchment, copies of which were presumably for sale. It was written in a mock-gothic script:

> This is Thomas Becket, son of a Norman merchant and "holy blissful martyr" of the legend. His story has been presented as a classic struggle between Church and State, between gentle spirituality and integrity and brute power. A closer look shows it to have been more a struggle between two arrogant and single-minded men, loving friends and raging enemies by turns, who fought out their personal quarrels on the field of history and made a thorough nuisance of themselves doing it.
>
> The story is far from heroic. Everything that happened could have been avoided with a bit of common sense and it led to a climax that was as unnecessary as it was predictable. . . .

The thing droned on, but you get the idea. I recalled what Dr. Happy Harry Cox had said, after imparting his litany of esoterica: "If you were never a special person, you are a special person now."

So many of us are special persons now, prepared to shrug off at a moment's notice the frumpy frock of common knowledge for the hip Nehru jacket of revisionism. It's the quickest way to be thought independent of mind, impervious to hogwash, above the herd, an initiate . . . a *special person*. Once no dorm room decor was complete without the black-and-white bumper sticker (still seen, once in a while, through a cloud of exhaust, faded and peeling from the rear of aged Volvos or VW buses) that told us to "Question Authority." Nobody stops there any more. The authority of common knowledge is to be routinely denied. For enlightened baby boomers—and who among us is not enlightened?—revisionism is a habit of mind.

The habit informs everything. It's a rare suspense movie these days in which the affable government agent, once Hollywood's pillar of virtue, doesn't reveal himself as the psychopathic villain. (Hollywood still thinks of this as a trick ending.) Journalism, too: the hippest editor craves a piece proving that what you thought to be history is actually bunk. A recent issue of a national art magazine, for example, alerted us to the "Gauguin myth." Initiates now know that the French painter, who we thought created charming works in a South Seas idyll, in truth led a shabby life racked with disease on a Tahiti which, having long before his arrival abandoned native ways, lacked only a Pizza Hut to complete its descent into Western decadence. Those lovely native robes? Of European design. And the lubricious maidens? Hookers. And the exotic Tahitian titles Gauguin chose for his paintings? Ungrammatical, betraying a tourist's knowledge of the language. The paintings themselves were derivative to the point of piracy. A splendid piece, a paradigmatic piece: everything you know about Gauguin is wrong.

The smart guy is the one who's wised up to the con, in its infinite forms. Taught so many truths as a schoolboy (and so timid then, so cowed by the Gilbert Stuart portrait of Washington poised magisterially above the chalkboard!), he presumes as an adult that not one of them can survive the scrutiny of the wake-up-and-smell-the-coffee mind, the eye from which the scales have fallen. In the hands of baby boomers, any book, any movie, any scholarly treatise, any conversation might at any moment transmogrify into a game of oneupsmanship: how big a truth can you topple? "Did you know that our forefathers took drugs?" Dr. Cox asks, introducing a newsreel called "Ben Franklin: Hero or Hophead?" And so: the Iwo Jima memorial—a monument to heroism? Get wise. Becket and Henry—an epochal clash of Church and State? Puh–*leeze.*

By embracing revisionism, the baby boomers make themselves heirs to an honored tradition. The first debunker, it might even be said, was Tacitus, who in the *Annals of Imperial Rome* portrayed the much-admired Tiberius as a bloodthirsty hypocrite. In America, debunking has more often been the business of misanthropes: Mark Twain pooh-poohing the charge up San Juan Hill, Ambrose Bierce reducing the Civil War to simple man-to-man barbarism, H. L. Mencken setting the record straight on the Gettysburg Address ("It is difficult to imagine anything more untrue"). From this distance the practice seems refreshing, in a democratic sort of way. The debunker has historically been thought of as the skunk at an insufferably starchy garden party we wouldn't mind crashing ourselves. And complicated truths are always the more deeply satisfying. Whose Lincoln holds the greater appeal—Carl Sandburg's saint, or the tortured politician of the Sandburg-slaying Edmund Wilson?

Every boomer should feel flattered to be placed in the company of Tacitus, of course, but every boomer also knows that a lot has happened since Imperial Rome—Vietnam, Watergate—

and with the last generation revisionism became impulse, habit, reflex. As a matter of intellectual history, the origins of compulsive debunking lie in the triumph of scientism over religion. That victory is understood as a victory for sophistication and good character: the man devoted to the disinterested pursuit of truth beats back the sap seduced by wishful thinking. The easy discrediting of biblical revelation filled the smart guys with a giddy confidence from which the culture has never quite recovered. It is this strain of revisionism that the boomers are heir to, and which they have assumed as their attitude toward the world. The compulsion to debunk has trickled down; it is a long, winding distance from Henry Mencken to the skeptic on the greensward around the Iwo Jima memorial.

One of the pools where this trickle gathers and eddies is a genre of pulp books dedicated explicitly to the proposition that everything you know is wrong, with titles like *The Prevalence of Nonsense; Legends, Lies & Cherished Myths of American History; They Never Said It; Fabulous Fallacies; Popular Fallacies;* and so forth. The best-selling *Legends, Lies, etc.*, by a television news reporter, is the most recent of these. Its jacket copy could have been written by Happy Harry Cox himself: pilgrims never lived in log cabins; no one ever died in a frontier shootout at high noon; independence wasn't declared on July 4. The author's foreword begins: "Americans . . . know that the Pilgrims landed on Plymouth Rock, that Teddy Roosevelt charged up San Juan Hill, that Columbus discovered the world is round, and that Eli Whitney invented the cotton gin. The punch line, of course, is that Americans know all these things but that none of these things are true." It's a punch line that you can see coming (of course) a mile away.

Not surprisingly, these collections and their manna of truth begin to stale with time. Bergen Evans's pathbreaking collection of the '40s, *The Natural History of Nonsense*, devotes several pages to refuting beliefs in mermaids, wolves that raise children, conception without coition, and other "vulgar errors." In attempting to free us from the "barbarism and slavery" of common wisdom, however, Bergen casts rather a wide net, hauling up some items that would strike a less astringent mind as harmless: it's not true, he insists, that "there are no atheists in foxholes"—a bit of conceptual slavery, commonly assumed during World War II, that he refutes by citing the testimony of unbeliever s who actually huddled in foxholes and emerged with their secular humanism intact. Further, Evans notes, people still believe (you can hear the chains clank) that holding to twenty-one as the legal age of majority is something other than superstition. (And it is, by the way: it's tradition. The debunker considers tradition more treacherous than superstition, though formally indistinguishable from it. Tradition is the vessel of the vulgarest errors, and so must be dismissed with brutal finality. Perhaps you merely Question Authority, but you've got to come right out and Tell Tradition It's Full of Shit.)

Twenty years after Bergen Evans disposed of the scurrilous canard about foxholes, Ashley Montagu and Edward Darling reopened the issue in *The Prevalence of Nonsense*, published in 1967. Careful examination of source materials confirmed Evans's finding: the belief is "nonsense." Montagu and Darling pressed ahead with the business of dismantling the edifice of bushwa, ticking off the lies with clinical dispatch. The apple never fell on Newton's head. Fulton's boat wasn't called the *Clermont*. Mussolini did not make the trains run on time. Eating less salt has no effect on health. Bloodthirsty spectators at the Colosseum never called for the death of a vanquished combatant by turning thumbs down (although I've heard they invented the wave).

Beneath this clutter, Montagu and Darling found deeper misapprehensions choking the brain of *Homo sapiens*, particularly the brain of the American bourgeois circa 1967—who, they conceded, was a "potentially brilliant creature." Manipulated by dark forces, constantly lied to, he believed such "outrageous nonsense" as "the proverbial saying that the man who works hardest gets the greatest rewards," and that "warfare can be morally justified under certain circumstances," and (even!) that he is "less superstitious than [he] used to be, far less primitive." Now to debunk this last bit of nonsense might seem to undermine the debunking enterprise itself. And indeed, though Montagu and Darling affirm their dedication to the manful exposure of untruth, "we do so without entertaining the alluring whimsy that to expose it will end it." Ignorance, they know, survives them. To no whimsy—not even the notion that he might be doing some good—does the debunker succumb. A failure, then, but a noble one.

As it turns out, Montagu and Darling were (forgive me) wrong, for they published their book just as that unprecedented carnival of debunking, the baby boom, was unpacking its tent. The main attractions were gaudy and numberless: books, magazine articles, movies, plays, and television shows. But very few of them were tempered by Montagu and Darling's sense of resignation and futility. The new zeal was the zeal of the reformer, confident in his high purpose; for revisionism now aimed not simply at correcting factual errors but at moral improvement, too. One of the most popular movies of the day, *Little Big Man*, starred Dustin Hoffman as a dwarfish picaro who dragged us for our own good through an Old West unknown to devotees of the Duke and John Ford. The truth could at last be told, clear-eyed and unsentimental, and it was a moral truth. Here the white man was avarice and hypocrisy made flesh, animated by a perplexing need to mutilate women and children. Dustin met a cavalry officer: an unshaven Visigoth. Dustin met Wild Bill Hickok: a neurotic has-been. Dustin met a frontier preacher: a gluttonous sadist, married to a slut.

Little Big Man's Indians, by contrast, were so *gentle* . . . so close to the earth. Sex was free; homophobia unknown; and the occasional toke was salubrious, even ceremonial. Cheyenne villages, in fact, were indistinguishable from any number of communes nestled at that very moment in the Sierra Nevada, peopled by dropouts from UC–Santa Cruz. As the cameras panned the inside of a tepee you half expected to see well-thumbed copies of Kahlil Gibran lying about. And this idyll was destroyed in a river of blood by an icon of prerevisionist America: George Armstrong Custer, psychopath. (Rivers of blood, then as now, were good box office.) Hermetically sealed in a two-and-a-half-hour Hollywood movie, the debunking afforded no argument. When in the end Custer fell at Little Big Horn—"Custer had it coming" read a bumper sticker of the day—the audience cheered, as I recall. I was with my high school history class at the time.

Soon afterward, Gore Vidal began his series of entertaining but faintly ridiculous historical novels. (The series has multiplied so fruitfully that Gore now calls himself "America's biographer.") Gore Vidal's America is irremediably debased by the slithery forces of commerce, the cravings of captains of industry, the bumbling of buffoonish pols; a dim-witted populace meanwhile plays the pawn, lullabied by the same fairy tales Gore hopes to debunk. It is revealing of his method that he chose Aaron Burr as the subject of his most entertaining (and ridiculous) romance. In *Burr*, the founding of America is told through one of America's most cynical men. Gore admits, in the novel's coy epilogue, that he thinks rather more highly of Thomas Jefferson than does his hero, but for the most part the reader is to take Burr's appraisals as accurate. And who wouldn't? They're so different, so daring, so *fresh!*

Here, for example, is our first glimpse of George Washington: "I looked up into his face: the yellow pockmarked skin was slightly covered with powder; the gray eyes sunk in cavernous sockets were lustreless; the expression was grave but somewhat vacant." Moreover, "he had the hips, buttocks, and bosom of a woman." These are the truths Gilbert Stuart dared not tell. And if the Washington packaging was unpleasant, the insides were worse: Washington throughout proves himself vain, willful, an oaf on the battlefield and a nonstarter in bed, infinitely susceptible to flattery, ill-spoken—pockmarks of the soul. One by one the heroes fall: Jefferson, Hamilton, Clay. The particulars change, but the gravamen of Gore's indictment doesn't. "History, as usual," Burr writes, "has got it all backward."

The Founding Fathers routinely take it on the chin from the debunker; the first roundhouse was delivered seventy-five years ago by Charles A. Beard, who famously argued that the delegates to the Constitutional Convention worked solely by the light of their own financial ledgers. Conflicts of interest tainted each roll call. The Constitution, Beard said he had proved, was merely "an economic document drawn with superb skill" (the compliment is backhanded) by a "consolidated economic group . . . whose property interests were immediately at stake"; and by God (whom they didn't believe in, by the way), the fat cats meant to keep what they had and expand it, too. Each happy word choice in the great document, every carefully inserted clause, was money in the bank.

Beard's thesis is now mostly passed over by historians, but the professional debunker's passion for the old heroes never cools. Fawn Brodie's life of Thomas Jefferson, published in the early '70s, is surely the most successful debunking since Spencer Tracy lashed Fredric March to the witness stand in *Inherit the Wind*. Most of the claims of her rather loony biography have faded with time; but her tale about Jefferson and his love slave Sally Hemings is now indelibly part of his public portrait: Author of the Declaration of Independence, Founder of the University of Virginia, and Casanova of the slave quarters. No matter that revisionist enthusiasm alone inspired Fawn's case, since she lacked any supporting evidence. It's so *fresh*, so *now*, so *revealing*. . . .

Except that it isn't new. Word of the cross-racial dalliance was first circulated by a pamphleteer names James Callender, during Jefferson's first term as President. Callender's accounting of his betters is so suited to modern debunking that one wonders why he hasn't been cited by more of our revisionists. A century and a half before Gore, he pegged Washington as "a scandalous hypocrite"; John Adams, Callender decided, was a British spy (someone might want to check this out). But Fawn's revisionism is wrinkled by a curious anomaly. In alleging that the President had made a lover of a slave, Callender hoped to smear Jefferson; with the same allegation, Fawn hopes to pay him a compliment. Many modern debunkers say they're merely "humanizing" the subject at hand. The claim is almost always disingenuous, but Fawn really means it. When Jefferson chased Sally around the barnyard, he revealed himself, in Fawn's eyes, to be an eighteenth-century Hef, making Monticello the Playboy Mansion of the Old Dominion. Jefferson, Fawn writes, had "destroyed any lingering puritanical legacy from his childhood . . . and confirmed his private conviction that a man is master of his own body and may govern it as he pleases. . . . His vital sexuality . . . reasserted itself to make possible a new if hidden happiness." Of course, this was before AIDS.

If you want to prove everything you know is wrong, at least about America, there's no point in stopping with the Founders. Begin at the beginning, and the rest of the story almost tells itself. Thus debunkers pay particular attention to Christopher Columbus, and as the 500th anniversary of his voyage approaches (it *was* 1492, wasn't it?), the truth-telling will likely reach a deafening crescendo. Sure, he proved the world was round (did not) by discovering America (wrong), but he was also "a murderer, he was a slave trader, he was a rapist, he was the architect of a policy of genocide that continues today in this hemisphere." I quote the remarks of Glenn Morris, professor of the University of Colorado's department of political science, delivered in honor of Columbus Day 1989.

Professor Howard Zinn of Boston University opens his *People's History of the United States* with an engaging revision of every schoolboy's Columbus story. The pre-Columbian natives of Zinn's account, the Arawak, are supernally childlike, first cousins to Dustin Hoffman's Cheyenne. The men are agile, and great swimmers. Women give birth without pain. All dance naked by the firelight, and since, like Jefferson, they are masters of their own bodies, their promiscuity is unmarred by jealousy. But then the apocalyptic landfall: Columbus comes out swinging (an ax), lopping off hands and heads with that deft bloodlust peculiar to Europeans. Professor Zinn closes his first chapter; and the American story has begun.

Scholars of the academy like Zinn—I'll call him a scholar—face unremitting pressure to reject accepted wisdom. Professor B. J. Whiting of Harvard once formulated a principle of academic careerism: the easiest way for a scholar to advance is to seize a proposition that everyone knows to be true and pronounce it false. Whole departments of our great universities have been constructed according to Whiting's Law. Sometimes the method is a simple shift of emphasis: for adepts of Women's Studies, a firebrand named Elizabeth Cady Stanton looms larger in American history than Washington or Lincoln. Partisans of Ethnic Studies see the internment of Japanese-Americans as the defining event of World War II, overshadowing (and this is a gauntlet thrown at Women's Studies) even the critical contribution of WACS and Rosie the Riveter. Just as often, though, the rejection comes wholesale: it is central to the scheme of Biblical Studies, especially as taught in seminaries, that the authors of the Bible were deluded in every particular. Anyone enrolled in a "Bible as Literature" class now knows that Jesus wasn't born in Bethlehem. Professor Rudolph Bultmann gave new life to Biblical Studies when he coined the term "demythologize," denoting a method that encourages the scholar to reinterpret a biblical passage so that it comes to mean precisely the opposite of what it says. From here we take but a few short steps across the quad to Eng. Lit., where deconstructionists teach that no matter how we interpret the text, it has no meaning at all.

Crass ideology motivates much of this scholarship, it's true, but nobody should underestimate the demands of the tenure track. Rehearsing what we already know to be true is as death to a prof who hungers for an endowed chair. The dilemma is starkly simple: What on earth is he going to write about? Recently baby boom scholars who specialize in the history of the western United States have been aflame with revisionism, and not a moment too soon. The traditional view offered by Frederick Jackson Turner—that the western experience was formed by the uniquely American combination of individualism, free land, and protected property rights—held sway for so long that the field had been picked clean. But now a phalanx of Young Turks are busy burying Turner, and what might be called the Little Big Man thesis is in the ascendant. Art has imitated Life; Life has imitated Art; but never before has scholarship imitated a boffo box-office smash. Following Dustin Hoffman, Ph.D., scholars now assemble lustily to prove to one another that the Wild West was a manifestation of racism, sexism, and wanton disregard for fragile ecological balances—the Three Horsemen, in one scholar's words, of "conquest, exploitation, and environmental destruction." Ageism, too, enters in, with homophobia close behind, giving rise to a fresh round of seminars, conferences, monographs, tenure, fame. . . . Infinite theses to prove: There were no wagon trains! Calamity Jane read Sappho! Nobody played poker! The coffee tasted great! Myths to unveil, lies to expose! *Something to write about!* Thus, with a heaving sigh of relief, is scholarship reborn.

But it can get to be a strain, as poor Robert William Fogel will tell you. By the mid-'70s, Professor Fogel was already something of a superstar in the ever-widening revisionist circles, having announced—*pace* everybody—that railroads weren't a crucial factor in the development of the American West. It was a tough act to follow, and unexploded myths were getting scarcer. There were only a few hundred years of American history, after all, and thousands upon thousands of historians, scores of historians for every year (every month, it seemed like) of history, a crowded field, the bodies shoving and jostling for scraps, pittances. He wanted to write about slavery, but what was there about slavery that we didn't already know? The degradation, the squalor, the broken families, the unrewarded toil under a pitiless sun, the derangement of planters who would use their fellow men as chattel . . .

Wrong!

Professor Fogel calls himself a cliometrician, a historian who reconstructs history "on a sound quantitative basis." With the aid of census data and plantation ledgers and computer processing he formulated perhaps the most daring thesis in the history of history: *Slavery wasn't as bad as all that.* Of course, this proposition, like Miss Brodie's Jefferson-as-horndog thesis, wasn't terribly new: it had been articulated, in fact, by every champion of slavery since—well, since Columbus clamped the first studded collar on the first hapless Arawak.

Now, Professor Fogel and his colleague Stanley Engerman took pains to argue, convincingly, that they weren't racists. They insisted that their book *Time on the Cross* represented "the honest efforts of scholars whose central aim has been the discovery of what really happened." They were merely setting the record straight, hosing off our sticky sentimentality, trying to get us to cut the crap. The truth, then: the antebellum South was not an economic basket case but a boom region; slave agriculture was 35% more efficient (note the cliometrician's exactitude) than family farming; the typical slave, far from being exploited, received a 90% (precisely!) return on his labor, much more than industrial workers in the North; black slave families were only rarely broken up and were in truth encouraged by slave owners; the material condition of slaves compared favorably to that of urban workers and family farmers; and so on.

Their findings launched the authors on a tortuous path of argument, though they never lost sight of their revisionist destination. As it turns out, the only reason the rest of us have a negative view of slavery is that we inherited our view from the abolitionists, and abolitionists despised slavery because they were . . . *racists*—more odious, indeed, than slave owners, who at least thought highly enough of blacks to prize them as laborers.

Not at all incidentally, the effect of this conclusion is to shift blame for the sorry lot of some present-day blacks away from the legacy of slavery and the perniciousness of slave owners—those distant men we hold in contempt—onto the deceit of abolitionists, with whom most people today like to feel some identification. And if we praise these our heroes for their racism, then it follows that we too are racist. Thus, condemning slavery for its effect on American blacks is a racist act.

Extraordinary! In the annals of revisionism there is really nothing else quite like it. Utterly counterintuitive, subversive not only of common knowledge but of common morality, wholly irrational yet possessing an ineluctable interior logic, the Fogel-Engerman book achieved a kind of perfection in the art of revisionist one-upmanship. Reading *Time on the Cross*, you wonder: How could Fogel—how could anyone—top this?

He couldn't. From the dizzying heights to the crashing deep: it all went kaput. Fifteen years later, in 1989, Fogel published another book on slavery whose sad purpose was to retract many of the conclusions of *Time on the Cross*. Slavery, the post-Reagan Fogel decided, was a "profound injustice." As James McPherson pointed out in a review of the book in *The New Republic*, Fogel's new findings, after his earlier fireworks, sound almost banal—surely the lowest blow a critic can land on a professional debunker. "Slavery," Fogel now writes, "deserved to die despite its profitability and efficiency because it served an immoral end." Banal? He sounds, sometimes, like an abolitionist.

Frustrated readers will have noticed by now that I haven't addressed myself to the truth of the debunkers' various claims. Some *are* true: Mussolini never made the trains run on time. Some are false as a matter of record, like the faked Iwo Jima photograph and Professor Beard's account of the Founding Fathers; others only probably false, like the Jefferson-Hemings affair. Many are simply unfalsifiable, for they are not so much assertions as recastings, churlish attempts to trim the past according to a fashionably crabbed and bitter view of the present.

That unfalsifiability means we can't take heart from Professor Fogel's retreat. I see no weakening of the debunking impulse at large. If it were truly inspired by a desire to find out, as Professor Fogel wrote, "what really happened," it might slowly dissipate as individual assertions were meticulously disproved, assuming we could find someone who already had tenure to do the job. But inspiration for baby boom debunking is altogether different.

There is this consolation: the particularities of our present revisionism will pass from fashion by and by, and one day the baby boomers who pride themselves on a world-weary wisdom, their refusal to fall for the bullshit, will find the tables turned. A new generation of smart guys is being educated even now, soon to discover its own list of items for debunking. The task, though we don't like to think so, should not be difficult. Expect movies and paperbacks and symposiums. Watch for a biography asserting that Ringo was the genius behind the Beatles, and a monograph proving that Rosa Parks thought she *was* at the back of the bus; we'll read laboratory studies showing breakfast to be the least important meal of the day, and definitive testimony that Mother Teresa was a creep. How daring it will be, how new, how *fresh!* The constituents of Dr. Happy Harry Cox of Hellmouth, California, can no longer be denied.

Whatever Happened to Doris Day?

Bruce Bawer

*I*t happened all at once—or so at least it seemed to me at the time. Throughout my tender years, the movies as I knew them had been summed up in the single glorious and inviolate image of Doris Day. Yes, there were the wondrous, sentimental Disney cartoons, the most memorable being *Bambi* and *The Lady and the Tramp* (both of which my mother dutifully took me to see in re-release); there were the predictably dopey live-action Disney movies with such cutesy titles as *The Absent-Minded Professor* and *That Darn Cat!*; and there was *The Wizard of Oz*, which (like everyone else) I watched every year on CBS. But these were movies for *kids*, a distinction that we all understood at an early age. On the more grown-up end of the scale, there was (till 1962, anyway) Marilyn Monroe—but Norman Mailer hadn't yet gotten around to explaining to us her Cosmic Significance, and in any case my mother didn't take me to see Marilyn. She took me to see Doris.

To be sure, Doris frequently went under the name of Julie Andrews or Debbie Reynolds, and sometimes she even dyed her hair, acted a bit more genteel, and called herself Audrey Hepburn. But it was always Doris, perky and well-bred and whole-some, appealing but not coarsely seductive, often cosmopolitan but never rich or snooty, who personified the movies for me; it was Doris who sanguinely inhabited that respected territory between good-time girl and old maid (for the movies in those days made it clear to us that it was pitiful, if not disastrous, for a woman to be either), Doris who expertly fended off advances, in one congenial sex comedy after another, from the likes of Clark Gable, Cary Grant, and Rock Hudson (for the movies made it clear, too, that all men were by nature wolves, unless there was something wrong with them), Doris who elegantly and entertainingly managed the game of courtship in such a way that she would inevitably, at the end of the picture, win that man, that home, that wedding ring (for the movies made it clear that it was every woman's task to maneuver a good man into a marriage he may not have sought—which was, after all, for his own good as well as hers). And it was Doris, too, who time and again played the perfect middle-class American wife and mother—a doctor's wife (what else?) who'd sacrificed her singing career for husband and family in *The Man Who Knew Too Much* (1956); another doctor's wife who (again for husband and family) gave up her job as a TV-commercial pitchwoman in *The Thrill of It All* (1963).

Then, all at once—or, as I say, so it seemed to the late-baby boom child that I was—everything was different. Suddenly Elizabeth Taylor was getting a lot of attention for braying dirty words in *Who's Afraid of Virginia Woolf?* (1966). Suddenly there were movies playing in our local theater—foreign movies, *Danish* movies—that took lovemaking a good deal further than the ardent looks and merry badinage that passed between Doris and Rock in the first movie my mother had ever taken me to, *Pillow Talk* (1959). I didn't know much, at the time, about the events that formed the background to these developments: the rise of TV and the concomitant collapse of the studio system in Hollywood; the influence of Italian neorealism and of the French *nouvelle vague*, alongside whose finer fruits many of the products of Doris and company suddenly looked timid and synthetic; the slow disintegration of the once mighty censorial power of what had been called first the Hays Office and then the Breen Office (whose code had insisted, among other things, that even husband-and-wife characters couldn't share a bed, and that wrongdoing must always be punished by the last reel); the watershed event that was Maggie McNamara's employment of the formerly *verboten* word "virgin" in Otto Preminger's *The Moon Is Blue* way back in 1953. Nor did I realize that Doris herself had been the queen regnant of a transitional epoch in American motion pictures, that the remarkable combination of charm, wit, obsessively sophomoric naughtiness, and mawkish moralizing that had characterized so many of her pictures reflected a Hollywood in somewhat muddled passage from one way of rendering the world to another. Indeed, it took one further event—the rise to majority of the baby boom—to bring an end to the muddle and to deliver American movies to a New World's not-so-bright shores.

Landfall came with *The Graduate*. Upon its theatrical release in 1967, every teenager I knew went to see it at least once and talked about nothing else for weeks. And it *was* an entertaining picture. But what inspired such extraordinary enthusiasm on the part of these teens? Mostly this: *The Graduate* made a hero of someone close to their own age—a rare thing for an American movie to do in those days—and made dolts of the grownups. The movie laughed at the whole *idea* of being a grownup (a responsible one, anyway), laughed at the whole idea of making a career, of becoming a useful part of The System.

The most famous line in *The Graduate*—perhaps the most famous line in any movie of the '60s, for that matter—is the one-word bit of unsolicited career advice given by a helpful Southern-California-businessman party guest to Dustin Hoffman's just-graduated-from-Harvard Benjamin: "Plastics." The line got a big laugh way back then from the picture's baby boom audience, and it continues to get big laughs every time a couple of hundred baby boomers pack into a revival house to see the movie again. And in context, the line is sort of amusing. But not *that* amusing. The laugh's supposed to be on the businessman for pronouncing the word in such a reverential whisper: imagine thinking about plastics this way, imagine consecrating your life to it! But what, one must ask, has Benjamin got planned that's so much better? Sure, he's brilliant, or so we're told—but what sign does he show of it? He never says or does or creates anything brilliant. He floats in the family swimming pool. He responds with numb condescension to the compliments of his parents and their friends, all of whom consider him a Golden Boy. He's empty, anomic, uninspired. Who *better* to spend a lifetime in plastics? Besides, plastics was the sort of field in which you could've imagined Doris working in one of her career-gal roles. (After all, she'd worked with computers in *That Touch of Mink*, at a pajama factory in *The Pajama Game*, in advertising in *Lover Come Back*.) And if plastics was good enough for Doris, why wasn't it good enough for Dustin?

But the army of Prosperity Children who lined up for *The Graduate* didn't see it that way. Endlessly pampered by their Depression Children parents—by dads who were earning several times more than their dads ever had, by homemaker moms who had diligently read their Dr. Spock—these kids, the most privileged generation in the history of the world, were now in their teens and had begun to feel that movies should not be about people like their folks (who were, in any case, staying home and watching TV most of the time now) but should be for and about *them*. Like Benjamin—and like most young people raised in peace and comfort and abundance—these baby boomers believed fervently in their own importance, believed in their superiority to the bourgeois modalities which had helped make that peace and comfort and abundance possible, and believed, too, that the movies should reflect their own ready-made, glibly seditious attitudes about life, love, and the world around them. Never mind that those attitudes were jejune and narcissistic, and that these kids didn't really know a damn thing about the world around them. *The Graduate* made money. Those kids, rewarding it generously for its implicit endorsement of their *Weltanschauung*, made it the highest-grossing picture since *The Sound of Music* two years earlier. And they made Dustin (no Captain von Trapp, he) a star.

A star! America had never seen anything like it. For Dustin wasn't anything like Doris's leading men. He was not only no Captain von Trapp; he was no Gable, no Grant, no Hudson. Dustin was short, Dustin was homely, Dustin didn't know how to dress or make scintillating small talk, Dustin was congenitally awkward and unsuave. But suddenly that didn't seem to matter anymore. Suddenly the movies as they had been were fading fast. The reception of pictures like *The Graduate* had helped Hollywood producers to realize that the grown-up audience for theatrical films had diminished dramatically, and that there was therefore a smaller market than ever before for Doris Day-type fare, let alone for the sort of literate comedies and dramas in which actresses like Bette Davis, Katharine Hepburn, Jean Arthur, Irene Dunne, and Rosalind Russell had once starred. No, the target audience for theatrical films now consisted principally of young people—namely, the overpopulated, overindulged, just-edging-out-of-their-minority baby boomers, who had more leisure time and pocket money than any previous generation of American youngsters, who were more *aware* of themselves as a generation, and who were unabashedly eager to see themselves celebrated on the screen, their life-styles glorified, their manners and morals lionized. So it was that a star such as Julie Andrews turned anachronistic overnight, her manner being simply too decorous, her appearance too tidy, and her singing voice too removed in timbre from that insolent Jim Morrison/Janis Joplin raspiness for the comfort of many baby boomers. And so it was, too, that Doris (herself no Janis Joplin) hastily effected, in 1968, an escape to TV.

And just in time too, for the next year saw not only the return of Dustin in *Midnight Cowboy*—the first A-budget picture to get an X rating, and the first X-rated picture to win an Academy Award for Best Picture of the Year—but the advent of Peter

Fonda and Dennis Hopper in *Easy Rider*. The scuzzy, undomesticated protagonists of these pictures could hardly have been more different from polished gents like Clark Gable and Cary Grant. And that, of course, was the whole idea: these were characters that baby boomers could "identify with." They were "free." They'd "dropped out" of a corrupt society, a *plastic* society. Yet what did they have to offer in its place? "Do your own thing," they said. Yet in these movies, and others like them, they were all doing exactly the same thing: goofing off, abusing controlled substances, wandering aimlessly across America. They claimed to be creating a new society, but they didn't put much serious thought into it. As Ned Rorem wrote at the time, "The freedom of the easy riders is no more self-questioning, no less assembly-line than the conformism of the fifty annual Miss America contestants." Pictures like *Easy Rider* didn't encourage independence on the part of their young viewers; they fostered imitation. They provided baby boomers with a dress code, a vocabulary, a primer of attitudes. And their arrival marked the beginnings of something else, too: a new, distinctly baby boomer attitude toward movies.

For *Easy Rider* and its ilk weren't primarily out to entertain. Weak on story and character and dialogue, they sought rather to embody the vapid slogans of Youth Culture, to epitomize the politically correct generational attitudes toward Life (which, for the baby boomers, generally meant life-style), toward Politics and Culture, toward War and Peace. And most baby boomers ate it all up. Had their parents, in the '30s and '40s, ever asked for or been served such shrill, facile fare? Not really. There *had* been stark, socially conscious pictures during the Depression (among them, of course, such estimable movies as *The Grapes of Wrath* and *I Am a Fugitive from a Chain Gang*), and during World War II there'd been the occasional flagrant piece of propaganda (such as Lillian Hellman's awful *The North Star*). But for the most part, moviegoers in the '30s and '40s didn't get or want strident, self-righteous politics or sociology in their movies.

And why would they have wanted them? During the '30s and '40s, the world was a tough place; moviegoers *knew* it was a tough place; they didn't need or want to be lectured about this state of affairs by, of all people, sheltered, affluent Hollywood writers and directors. In times of depression and war, what an affront that would have been! Movies (everybody knew) weren't serious, they were entertainments; life itself was too serious a proposition for movies to be taken seriously as a reflection of it. With the rare exception of a film like *Citizen Kane*, whose artistic ambition and extraordinary merit clearly placed it in another category altogether from the usual deft entertainments, serious-minded people didn't take movies *seriously*, as they did literature and the fine arts.

At the same time, however, moviegoers of the '30s and '40s did expect the movies themselves to take certain things—religion, chastity, and patriotism among them—very seriously. And justly so. For escaping temporarily from one's own life into the world of a movie didn't mean escaping from morality; it didn't mean renouncing, even for a moment, the ethical standards by which one lived that life. Nor did it mean being encouraged to sneer at intelligence, at culture, at the arts. On the contrary, the movies of the '30s and '40s consistently reflected an understanding that in the real world, real commitment, artistic, social, political, or otherwise, involved not only rhetoric but hard work and sacrifice. Philistine though those movies often were, they at least tended to bow respectfully whenever real art—or, for that matter, real greatness of any kind—came within their purview, erring (as they often did) in the direction not of scorn or ridicule but of a preposterous pietism (toward, for instance, Cornel Wilde's Chopin, Fredric March's Mark Twain, Greer Garson's Madame Curie, Paul Muni's Juarez). In those days, American movies routinely and unapologetically celebrated great men and women and their accomplishments.

Granted, the '30s and '40s were a time of prudish, reactionary production codes which made it impossible to tackle certain aspects of life honestly, and which, had those codes remained in effect in later decades, would have obstructed the production of some of the better films of recent years. Yet, for all their failings, these codes frequently (if unintentionally) served a constructive purpose: their very existence obliged writers and directors to find subtler, more elliptical—and therefore often more sophisticated and witty—ways of handling sex, violence, and the like than they might otherwise have chosen to adopt. (Check out the banter, for instance, in such movies as *The Palm Beach Story*, *His Girl Friday*, and *Mr. Blandings Builds His Dream House*.) Inadvertently, in other words, the censors' edicts strongly enforced the fundamental idea that art often lies in implication, sexual allure in suggestion.

By contrast, the rise to majority of the baby boomers ushered in an era of movies that were bluntly, numbingly literal-minded—movies often free of implication and explicit to the point of witlessness. Though increasingly candid about sex (displaying to us, in the "breakthrough" 1972 film *Last Tango in Paris*, a fat, aging Marlon Brando writhing nakedly atop Maria Schneider), the movies were robbed of sexiness; while increasingly graphic in their violence (showing us, in the "groundbreaking" 1974 picture *Death Wish*, the unprecedentedly brutal and bloody murder of Hope Lange, the very *image* of Doris), they came to depend, in many cases, more on sensationalism than on thoughtfully conceived emotional conflict for their dramatic impact. While movies ceased, moreover, to take such things as religion, chastity, and patriotism very seriously, baby boomers—who have always been good at being shallow about important things and deadly serious about frivolous things—began to take the movies themselves quite seriously indeed.

More and more frequently, as the '60s shaded into the '70s, baby boomers went to the movies looking not for dreams but for truths. But they didn't want just *any* truths: they wanted truths that flattered them, that were simple to digest, that didn't challenge their minds or assumptions, that confirmed their sense of their specialness and that confirmed also the corruption of the System, the emptiness of its values, and the awfulness of their parents (who, after all, personified that System, those values). Like so many turn-of-the-century American naturalistic novelists, moreover, the baby boomers often tended to equate truth with sordidness, with brutality, with inarticulateness. Wit? Fluency? Forms of oppression. High culture? Antidemocratic. Screenwriters who had written movies for decades found themselves being told, in the '70s, that their dialogue was "too uptown": too artful, too polysyllabic. Systematically, movie producers dumbed-down the flicks, purged them of regard for intelligence and sophistication. The handsome bourgeois heroes of earlier decades gave way to homely bohemian antiheroes; comely, cultured leading men largely evaporated from the scene (their breed continuing to be represented mainly by Redford and Newman), and in their place rose an army of Dustin Hoffmans, Elliott Goulds, Al Pacinos, and Jack Nicholsons. When well-dressed, well-bred, well-spoken, and well-adjusted citizens did surface in movies of the late '60s and '70s, it was generally as villains or fools; their very cultivation was understood to brand these men as sinister or silly.

The rules that these movies followed were in their own way as strict as those of the Breen and Hays offices: a hero could be a hooker (like Jon Voight in *Midnight Cowboy* or Jane Fonda in the 1971 *Klute* or Richard Gere in the 1980 *American Gigolo*) but never an artist; he could be a borderline psychopathic patient in a state mental hospital (like Jack Nicholson in the 1974 *One Flew Over the Cuckoo's Nest*) but never a physician or research scientist in the same hospital. If you *did* dare to make a movie about something as hoity-toity as, say, a classical composer, you had to be sure to make a total jerk out of him, as Tom Hulce did with Mozart in *Amadeus* (1984), or else worry that nobody would like him. Likewise, if you had a character who was identified in any way with the System—say, a senatorial candidate (like Redford in the 1972 *The Candidate*), a detective (Nicholson in the 1974 *Chinatown*), or a CIA agent (Redford in the 1975 *Three Days of the Condor*)—you had to be sure that by the end of the picture he was thoroughly disenchanted with the whole shooting match. But it was even better to have as a hero somebody who was completely at odds with the System, however inane (or even insane) his reasons for his opposition, however barbarous his means of enacting it. There had always been movies that made heroes of gentlemen burglars and the like (*Raffles*, *The Law and the Lady*, *To Catch a Thief*), but now we were given a spate of pictures celebrating truly murderous, amoral criminals, most prominently *Bonnie and Clyde* (1967) and *The Godfather* (1972).

Even as all these outrageous new ethical guidelines were taking hold in Movieland, baby boomers who'd gone off to college were learning from their hipper humanities professors (many of whom had been specially trained in that brave new discipline known as Popular Culture) that film (not "movies" any more) was *the* art form of the century, precisely because it was the most populist art form. Its potent accessibility, they explained, was its glory; the fewer barriers a film placed between itself and the Common Man, the better. Yet these profs—and, within a few years (and in far greater numbers), their baby boom pupils—took to explicating some of the more uncomplicated specimens of this most accessible of genres as if they were as intricately layered with meanings as *Hamlet*. Periodicals with titles like *Sight and Sound*, *Film Literature Quarterly*, and *Cinema Journal* soon littered the academic landscape. And as baby boomers themselves gradually advanced into the august ranks of the pop-culture professoriate, film study came to be taken for granted as a serious intellectual discipline, and its pipe-smoking, tweed-wearing practitioners, who applied their critical gifts to sober, heavily footnoted essays on such subjects as "The 'Liberated' Heroine of Recent Hollywood Films" and "Woody Allen's Comic Use of Gastronomy," came to be accepted as legitimate educators alongside the professors of classics and history.

What's important here is that those footnote-heavy essays

reflected more than just a reaction to academic publish-or-perish pressures: they mirrored a new baby boomer seriousness about movies. It was a seriousness that was reflected, more prominently, in the writings of Pauline Kael, who, after being hired as a regular film critic by *The New Yorker* in 1967, quickly became to many moviegoing "intellectuals" of the baby boom generation rather what Edmund Wilson had been to their more literary-minded counterparts of a generation earlier. In her long, intense, often spontaneous-seeming reviews, Kael enthusiastically endorsed off-the-cuff experimental movies like Robert Altman's *McCabe and Mrs. Miller* (1971), *Thieves Like Us* (1974), and *Nashville* (1975) for their crude vitality, while condemning more literate and accomplished films for their excessive polish and professionalism—thereby lending a profound air of legitimacy to the already widespread baby boom preference of spontaneity to craft, of the visceral to the intellectual, of the raw to the *raffiné*. The staid columns of *The New Yorker* and the suppleness of her own prose helped to disguise the degree to which Kael's terms of praise and putdown were, in the annals of serious criticism, genuinely grotesque. While Julie Andrews (as Kael declared in a typical critique) was "infuriatingly sane," Nick Nolte was an "ideal screen actor" because of his "rough edges," and Matt Dillon excelled because, having absolutely no acting techniques to encumber him, he allowed viewers to "feel they're in direct contact with this luminous kid." Altman, one of her favorite directors, earned this honor by being "recklessly original"; similarly, a movie won her praise for its "likable sloppiness." Reckless, rough, sloppy, uncivilized: in Kael's lexicon, such words were the chief terms of praise.

Though herself no baby boomer, Kael vividly mirrored baby boomer tastes and assumptions and in turn exerted an extraordinary influence upon the ways in which baby boomers, in the '70s and '80s, came to think and talk about movies. Kael had a lot to do, in fact, with the widespread repudiation by baby boomers of the distinction between movies and high culture: if there had been a time when one was expected to know something about current poetry, theater, and art in order to be recognized as a serious cultured person, there came a time when all that one had to do was to be able to quote Pauline Kael on the latest James Bond picture. In bestowing *The New Yorker* badge of seriousness upon even the junkiest of pop movies—movies about which, time and again, she wrote in rhapsodic tone and at an epic length that would be more appropriate to a critical discussion of, say, Proust—Kael freed a million upwardly mobile baby boomers from the oppressive notion that they had to know anything about *real* culture to be intellectually respectable. It should be no surprise, then, that Kael served as *the* model for many of the baby boom generation's most influential movie critics.

How things were changing! Hollywood had always made movies about young people—but never had there been so many, and never had they *glorified* young people so much. Andy Hardy had, after all, always learned his lessons from Judge Hardy, not the other way around. And he'd hardly been looked upon as representative of a generation. That was what was different now: the baby boom was the first generation to have movies made about it, as such. And invariably there was less self-criticism in these movies than there was self-celebration. For, cynical and irreverent as baby boomers have always been about everything else, no generation has ever been more brazenly sentimental about itself, about the trashy pop-culture totems of its common childhood, and about its solemnly proclaimed "idealism." Lawrence Kasdan's slick, dishonest *The Big Chill* (1983) gave baby boomers a chance to wax nostalgic about their erstwhile hippiedom—but despite the film's pretense of engagement with ideas about baby-boomerdom, it was essentially an empty orgy of generational self-love and self-congratulation. There was little moral exploration in *The Big Chill*, little attempt to find meaning in the characters' metamorphoses from young rebels into upstanding citizens in their thirties. Mainly the movie exuded an infantile sense of wonder: "Wow!" it appeared to be saying, "We've turned into grownups! And we're *mortal!* Aren't we remarkable!" This shallow picture struck as forceful a note with baby boomers as *Easy Rider* had done fourteen years earlier; and if the earlier movie had seemed to reflect a romantic conceit that baby boomers were the first generation ever to go through puberty and have sex, so *The Big Chill* likewise seemed to reflect an equally romantic conceit that they were the first generation ever to settle down with marriages, houses, careers, and children of their own.

The baby boomers' highly vocal existence had helped induce Hollywood to gear its movies largely toward their sensibilities. But as the '70s melted into the '80s, movies increasingly became directed toward an even younger generation—namely, toward the baby boomers' own small sons and daughters. Having abandoned the adult for the teenage audience in the late '60s, Hollywood turned ten or fifteen years later to the even younger preteen market. And these movies were largely the products of baby boom writers, directors, producers, and studio executives —people who (unlike their counterparts of old) had grown up on TV and talkies and consequently appeared to comprehend life, to a disturbing extent, in rudimentary visual terms.

Accordingly, it was the distinctively filmic virtues that tended to receive the most attention in these movies. Almost invariably, baby boom moviemakers (many of whom were graduated from film schools) are masters of film technique; but their ability to write (or at least select) good scripts is far less impressive. They don't seem to realize the importance of a well-written script, don't seem to know anything about dramatic construction, don't seem capable of telling good dialogue from bad. The sure grasp of dramaturgical rules that one used to be able to count on in major-studio movies is nowadays largely absent from all but the very best Hollywood films; perhaps even harder to find are successful screenwriters who have a feel for language, who can write dialogue as clever and playful and literate as that which Anita Loos, Billy Wilder, Ben Hecht, and Preston Sturges (among many others) once did. It's astonishing: whereas studio

chiefs once sought out the talents of the foremost serious novelists and playwrights, nowadays baby boomers who have never
even *read* anything serious can enjoy highly successful careers as
scriptwriters. And whereas the effectiveness of movies once re-
lied mainly on compelling, well-thought-out, and cleverly written stories about human relationships, it now often depends quite
heavily on wide-screen location cinematography, on loud Dol-
byized rock scores, and on special effects courtesy of International Light & Magic. With the advent of baby boomer
moviemakers, the dramatic content of American movies—and,
therefore, the *human* content, the *conceptual* content—has with-
ered drastically.

One has the impression, at times, that the minds of most
baby boom moviemakers have been expertly trained to process
nothing but images. At least one obvious reason, in fact, why
these moviemakers so often execute elaborate "homages" to their
celebrated predecessors (a practice pioneered largely by pre-
boomer Peter Bogdanovich in such efforts as the 1972 '30s-style
screwball comedy *What's Up Doc?*) is that they don't really have
sensibilities of their own. When a baby boomer movie does get
political, moreover, what it customarily amounts to is a dose of
facile, Politically Correct piety about race, war, gender, Big
Business, nuclear power, the environment. Often these movies
come accompanied by powerful visceral imagery (the battle
scenes in *Platoon*) and peace movement nostalgia (Joan Baez singing "Amazing Grace" at the end of *Silkwood*). But they tend to
originate less from a genuine sense of political commitment than
from a desire on the moviemakers' part to assume a fashionable
posture of "sensitivity" (which often means insensitivity to
thoughtful distinctions); and if they have a clearly defined goal,
it would apparently be less to shed light on the human condition
than to give baby boom filmgoers a chance to feel virtuous. Indeed, in an era when concerts, picnics, Hands Across America-
type displays, and Sunday afternoon marches down Fifth
Avenue are regarded as serious political acts, attending movies—

certain movies, anyway—likewise often qualifies, in enlightened baby boom circles, as a manifest demonstration of liberal virtue.

Yet baby boomer liberalism is a frivolous affair. In the average baby boomer-made film, there's little sense that anything is worth striving for except fame, sex, money, and athletic victory. One movie after another—among them John Hughes's *Ferris Bueller's Day Off* and Paul Brickman's *Risky Business*—presents, with patent admiration and with only the most superficial irony, a hero who combines a reckless, narcissistic, *Easy Rider*-ish antipathy toward bourgeois norms and obligations with a frank appetite for bourgeois comforts. Nor is there much evidence in contemporary movies of a curiosity about history. (How, after all, *could* history be interesting? *We* weren't there.) While the '30s and '40s saw hundreds of historical dramas being produced, hardly any baby boomer-created movies are set in earlier time periods, unless the protagonist travels there by means of a wacky time machine. Meanwhile, there are comedies galore—generally in the *Meatballs-Stripes-Caddyshack* vein—but little wit; as a rule, their humor is banal and empty and visual, aimed at childish minds, lacking in the charm and cleverness of such typical '30s and '40s comedies as *Ninotchka*, *The Women*, *The Awful Truth*, or *The Philadelphia Story*.

Many of the top baby boom directors have a knack—or at least a penchant—for fantasy and adventure. And some of their movies in these genres are truly wonderful of their kind. But others—such as *Gremlins*, *Goonies*, *Jaws* and its sequels, and the *Ghostbusters* and *Rocky* series—reach a level of aggressive stupidity, of calculated sameness, that few A movies of the '30s and '40s did. When baby boom moviemakers, moreover, try to do sophisticated romantic comedy or "realistic" drama, the results *(When Harry Met Sally, Empire of the Sun)* tend to be insipid, even embarrassing. You get the feeling that whenever these folks venture beyond the puerile they're on alien territory. What's more, if the movies of the '30s and '40s often made heroes out of men and women (Zola, Edison, Lincoln) who had made lasting contributions to mankind, today's movies are more likely to glorify the accomplishments of teenage black belts *(Karate Kid)* and exceptional bartenders *(Cocktail)*. On the very rare occasion when high culture does enter into the equation, it's generally extolled for shallow baby boom-style reasons: in *Dead Poets Society*, for instance, poetry is celebrated not for its beauty but for its ability to improve our life-styles by spurring us to action (poetry is, in other words, News You Can Use).

Ironically, films of the '30s and '40s which nobody took seriously at the time are now frequently looked upon by baby boomers as if they were high culture. PBS routinely airs such movies as *It's a Wonderful Life*, as well as gossipy documentaries about the lives of old movie stars such as Gregory Peck and Spencer Tracy; the promotional copy and introductory materials associated with these telecasts would have us believe that these motion pictures and performers comprise the chief monuments of American civilization. (Yet who doubts that if Peck and Tracy came along now, they'd have to content themselves with careers in dinner theater?)

That Steven Spielberg is, unarguably, the foremost movie director of the baby boom generation is supremely fitting. There's a lot to be said for movies like *Close Encounters* and *E.T.* and *Raiders of the Lost Ark*. But what all these pictures reflect is an extraordinary indifference to the comic and dramatic possibilities of adult life. That Spielberg chose, for example, to make a hero rather than a laughingstock of the pathologically regressive young husband and father in *Close Encounters* was astonishing enough; that so many baby boomers joined Spielberg in identifying with this character was truly bizarre. Spielberg's preoccupation, here and in his other big-box-office movies, with childhood dreams of outer-space visitors and with preposterous, boyishly imagined feats of derring-do is so romantic and obsessive that it would have unsettled Rousseau. These are children's movies for grownups; and their well-nigh unparalleled popularity among baby boomers makes it clear that baby boomers *want* children's movies. Perhaps even more influential than Spielberg, among fellow baby boom (and post-boom) directors, is the redoubtable John Hughes, who during the past several years has specialized in inane films about high school children. These pictures, which include *Pretty in Pink*, *Sixteen Candles*, *The Breakfast Club*, and *Ferris Bueller's Day Off*, represent an eerie accomplishment: the work of a man who seems completely (and quite happily) in sync with the mentality of a fifteen-year-old, and who apparently feels no compulsion to bring grown-up ironies or insights (à la *The Catcher in the Rye*) to bear. Hughes is, indeed, a perfect symbol of what would appear—so far, anyway—to be the baby boom's principal cinematic legacy to the generations that follow: namely, a consummate and abiding immaturity.

Second Childhood

John Podhoretz

*I*n 1981, the secretive Hollywood director Steven Spielberg began working on a movie called *A Boy's Life*. Little was known about the production, but Spielberg had spoken frequently of his desire to make a modern-day version of the old "Our Gang" short subjects, the slapstick live-action cartoons that featured hapless boys and girls performing in Keystone Kops style. *A Boy's Life*, Hollywood insiders thought, was that movie. Since Spielberg's previous foray into slapstick comedy, *1941*, had been an unmitigated disaster, *A Boy's Life* seemed a foolhardy project. It therefore generated little interest or excitement.

As it turned out, the title "A Boy's Life" was a deliberate subterfuge, intended to provoke as little interest as possible. The movie released a year later bore the title *E.T., the Extraterrestrial*, and it eventually made nearly $500 million. But despite Spielberg's decision to name the movie after the titular dwarflike alien with the glowing finger, his working title was actually more appropriate. The real strength and power of *E.T.* derives from its fully realized vision of a present-day American boy's life. In fact, *E.T.* is a cultural apotheosis of American boyhood in the age of the baby boomer; one would have to return to earlier times, to Booth Tarkington's *Penrod* or Mark Twain's *Tom Saw-*

yer, to find a portrait of childhood that struck so resonant a chord in American audiences.

The theme of *E.T.* is the spiritual greatness and moral superiority of children and childhood, in contrast to the spiritual aridity and moral inferiority of the adult world. In the world of *E.T.*, childhood and adulthood are at spiritual war. At best, the adults of *E.T.* are confused, at sea, unable to help themselves or others; at worst, they consciously seek to destroy all that is pure and noble. In Spielberg's fable, adults have forgotten the simple truths that every child knows. And when the child finally triumphs over the adults, it is the victory of good over evil.

Elliott, the hero of *E.T.*, is a serious and sober nine-year-old boy with a younger sister and an older brother. He lives in a Southwestern suburb in an elaborate and beautiful house that testifies to the affluence of his parents and the material ease of his existence. He has a circle of friends, imaginative boys with whom he tools around the neighborhood on his bike. This is not the image of the suburbs we got used to in the '60s and '70s, the drab and constricted life of Malvina Reynolds's song "Little Boxes," ironically praising the "little boxes made of ticky-tacky." Rather, it is an image closer to the cultural idealization of the '50s suburbs, "Father Knows Best" updated and made funky.

Father, however, is nowhere to be seen. He left his wife and family for a younger woman some months before the action of the movie begins. Elliott's mother (who goes unnamed) is a pretty and stylish woman in her early thirties, and has not taken her husband's desertion well. She is struggling; newly returned to the work force, and coping with her abandonment, she seems rather miserable but tries hard to keep a cheerful and competent disposition around her children. The children, particularly Elliott, seem to be made of sterner stuff than their mother. They are handling the divorce far better than she is; the daughter nonchalantly mentions their father's new girlfriend before being hushed violently by her brothers.

That image of emotional incompetence is as good as adults

get from Spielberg. In the movie's opening scene, E.T. has crash-landed in his spaceship and is desperately fleeing a group of scientists. We see the men as the three-foot-tall E.T. sees them, no faces, only ominous height; we know one of them only by the key chain hanging from his belt. (In the credits, this character is called "Keys.") E.T. finds refuge in the toolshed behind Elliott's house. When Elliott hears scary noises in the toolshed and then comes upon E.T., he is only momentarily frightened. His innate wisdom leads him to the realization that E.T. is not of this world. The eagerness with which E.T. gobbles up the Reese's Pieces Elliott strews in his path convinces the little boy that the alien is friendly and that he needs protection and help to return home.

Once his brother and sister are in on the secret, the adventure really begins for Elliott: hiding all traces of E.T. from the adult world. Worried that his garrulous sister will blab about E.T. to their mother, he tells her in a patronizing tone, "Only little kids can see him." His sister, wise beyond her years, replies with a roll of the eyes and the words "Give me a break."

And yet Elliott is right and his sister is wrong. Later, a drunken E.T. is stumbling around the first floor of the house when Elliott's mother suddenly returns home in the middle of the day. E.T. totters around beside and behind her, but in her self-absorption she never sees him, nor even senses his presence.

Accepting the possibility of E.T.'s existence requires a leap of imaginative faith; if one is, like Elliott's mother, hamstrung and obsessed with the mundane daily world, one will not be able to see him. On Halloween, when E.T. wanders around openly, adults think he is a child in costume. It is, in fact, only in child-only settings like Halloween that E.T. is free.

When adults do accept his existence, they start thinking about vivisection. This is true across the board, from Elliott's science teacher to the crew of scientists who have been hunting for the alien. When, at last, the scientists track E.T. down, the might and wrath of the adult world is visited upon the children.

In violation of the Third Amendment, men in uniforms take over Elliott's house, strap both E.T. and Elliott down and start performing tests on them. Their intrusiveness is horrifyingly harsh, and succeeds in killing E.T. (a scene that provoked the largest onrush of audience tears since Jackie Cooper begged the man, "Please, Mister, don't shoot my dog").

The alien's resurrection follows apace, of course, after which the neighborhood boys swing into action. They help Elliott and E.T. escape the clutches of the evil adults. The rescue is successfully accomplished on the foremost vehicle in children's transportation, the bicycle (with some help in levitation from the alien). When E.T. finally departs for his home planet, the adults who have chased and tortured him, as well as the boy's incompetent mother, stand mute and in wonder as E.T. says his good-byes to the only humans who have treated him like a treasured guest—the children.

Competent children, evil or incompetent adults: this cultural portrait represented a real break from the prevalent image of children in the '70s, an image that demonstrated how unbalanced and odd baby boom culture of that decade really was. *The Exorcist*, released in 1973, was the first in what became a series of films that made demonic villains out of children. Now, *The Exorcist* is a story of demonic possession, and so its makers can hardly be faulted for making its devil a monster. But they have incorporated their devil in the body of a little girl. And since movies are a supremely realistic medium, what we actually see is not the devil in the guise of a little girl, but a little girl acting like the very devil himself. The image of childhood in *The Exorcist* is as nightmarish as Spielberg's image is worshipful.

Regan, a twelve-year-old girl, is a child of divorce who is neglected by her father and troubled by the signs of her approaching adolescence. The devil first appears to her in the guise of a stuffed animal. She begins to regress, wetting her bed like a small child. She hurls a friend of her mother's out a third-story window, slithers snakelike across the floor chasing after her governess and must finally be strapped down to her bed. When the devil at last takes complete possession of her, her face is a mottled, scarred parody of adolescent acne. She spews vomit at anyone who approaches her.

The Exorcist converted all the unpleasantnesses of childhood (bed-wetting, vomiting) and the discomforts of impending adolescence (skin troubles) into a terrifying image of diabolism. Every time her mother enters Regan's room, she trembles with fear; sick with grief, she is also aware that this creature in place of her beloved daughter may kill her.

After a harrowing series of events, one of Regan's exorcists actually beats the child up. The scene was a first, in a manner of speaking, but, unfortunately, would not be the last. At the end of *The Exorcist*, the devil is exorcised and Regan is saved (until the sequel, at least). Damien Thorn had nothing like Regan's good fortune when he made his first appearance in *The Omen*, another gigantic box-office success, released three years later. Unlike Regan, Damien is evil from his very inception; he is, in fact, the devil's child, the anti-Christ. Damien goes Regan one better; instead of killing his mother's friend, he kills his mother (or rather, adoptive mother; his birth mother was a donkey). Riding around on a tricycle, the five-year-old Damien pushes his mother off the landing above her living room and rides away blithely as she crashes to the floor below.

The film's conclusion goes *The Exorcist* one better (or worse) as well, for this time the child does not merely get beaten up. Instead, in one of the more sickening scenes ever recorded on film stock, the audience is incited to root for Damien's adoptive father—played by the authoritative and liberally good-hearted Gregory Peck—as he attempts to stab the five-year-old boy through the heart with a ceremonial dagger. "No, Daddy, please, Daddy," Damien whimpers, his arms pinioned to an altar and tears streaming from his eyes. Even though within the context of the film Damien is the devil incarnate, those words and that image—together with the image of Regan in *The Exorcist*—sent a strange and disturbing message: You'd better get your children before they get you.

These films were not the products of a cultural vacuum. They were part of a school of self-referential psychology and sociology popular among baby boomers that was more concerned with the spiritual health of America's parents than that of its children. Books of the time, like Ellen Peck's *The Baby Trap* and John Rothchild and Susan Wolf's *The Children of the Counterculture*, suggested that the act of raising children was a threat to the self-expression of their parents, particularly their mothers.

Fictional portraits of baby boom children were no more affectionate. Alison Lurie's 1974 novel *The War between the Tates* features a bit of the demonic itself in its description of fourteen-year-old Jeffrey Tate and his sister Matilda: "Jeffrey and Matilda were beautiful, healthy babies; charming toddlers; intelligent, lively, affectionate children. . . . Then, last year, when Jeffrey turned fourteen and Matilda twelve, they had begun to change: to grow rude, coarse, selfish, insolent, nasty, brutish and tall. It was as if she were keeping a boarding house in a bad dream, and the children she had loved were turning into awful lodgers— lodgers who paid no rent, whose leases could not be terminated. . . . Jeffrey is sullen, restless and intermittently violent. Matilda is sulky, lazy and intermittently dishonest. Jeffrey is obsessed with inventions and space; Matilda with clothes and pop music. Matilda is extravagant and wasteful; Jeffrey miserly and ungenerous."

So *E.T.* did represent a profound change in cultural attitudes toward American children. But what, exactly, was the image of childhood we got from Spielberg and *E.T.*? The image was etched on Henry Thomas's beautiful and grave face. His Elliott is as adult and sophisticated a little boy as can be imagined. Elliott and his siblings are possessed of large vocabularies —not to mention command of profanity—and are adept at most things. They keep the house and themselves clean, are adept at holding onto and managing secrets, and their society is good-natured, loyal, courteous, and true.

There is, in other words, almost no trace of the childhood that, in our more unsentimental moments, we all remember. We do not see here the hierarchical and Hobbesian world in which boys (and girls) play and live, a world in which the physically strong prey on the physically weak and the odd are ostracized with puritanical passion. Nor do we see the terror that little boys and girls experience when faced with unfamiliar and threatening circumstances (another Spielberg film, *Poltergeist*, played cannily on that terror by making the frightening tree outside a little boy's window come alive and by putting a real live monster in a child's closet). Nor is there evidence of the fundamental lack of control most little boys have over their emotions; with nothing to compare his experiences to, any ordinary little boy suffers most forms of change and disruption as though he were the lead character in a Verdi opera. He must look to his parents as pillars of stability in what seems a dangerously off-kilter and incomprehensible world.

But in the Spielberg universe, it is Elliott's mother who is barely in control of her emotions and looks to her children for comfort; they are sufficiently self-possessed to find comfort elsewhere, in their friends and in their aliens.

It is usually the case that movies about childhood and adolescence, if they are at all honest, are quite painful to watch (François Truffaut's *The 400 Blows* comes readily to mind) because they reveal not only the ways in which a child comes face to face with a cold and often hostile world but also how ill-equipped the child is to deal with its harshness.

But Spielberg saves Elliott from that kind of pain by suggesting that while the adult world is both hostile and unattractive, the universe beyond it is benign and wise. He further idealizes Elliott and his friends by turning them into little adults, full of adult virtues but still possessed of the sense of wonder and unclouded expressions that children have. They are wise in the ways of human guile but are themselves guileless. The genius of *E.T* is that it gives children something to aspire to—a self-possession they cannot themselves achieve—while at the same time giving adults a means by which to identify with the goings-on on screen.

Romanticization aside, however, Spielberg also touched a chord because his portrait of the demands placed upon Elliott and his friends by '80s America was starkly realistic. These are children of divorce, saddled with incompetent parents and expected in some way to rear themselves. Elliott's maturity mirrored a kind of false maturity and *ersatz* sophistication which pop sociologists were concerned that American children were being imbued with.

In several books published in the early '80s, Marie Winn's *Children without Childhood* and Neil Postman's *The Disappearance of Childhood* primary among them, a bizarre condition afflicting the American child was diagnosed. The rise in the number of working women, in tandem with the staggering divorce rate and the use of television as a babysitting and educational tool, meant that children had to grow up too quickly and make their own way without help from their parents. As a result, childhood itself was disappearing, and children were passing from innocence to damnation without ever going through experience.

This argument was part of a war between pop sociologists of the '80s and those of earlier decades, and represented a retrenchment in liberal attitudes toward the family. Texts that had been used in previous decades (by Ellen Peck and John Rothchild, among others) to make excuses for the loosening of traditional family bonds were now cited as proof that these bonds needed strengthening.

The most notable was Philippe Ariès's *Centuries of Childhood*, a highly flawed 1962 study which advanced the view that childhood was not the natural state of the human being between the ages of three and twelve, but was instead a social creation and convenience little more than two hundred years old, a derivative of Enlightenment philosophy.

Radical feminists and other social engineers of baby boom America used Ariès's research in the '70s to claim that the creation of "childhood" went hand in glove with the domestic enslavement of women. In other cultures and at other times in Western history, children had been vested with great responsibility and authority over their own actions; it was Jean-Jacques Rousseau's fault that women were forced to stay at home and mind the children, it turned out.

In the early '80s, however, pop sociologists like Winn and Postman turned that idea on its head. The "invention" of childhood, they argued, was one of the hallmarks of a just and liberal society, and if childhood was today in danger of "disappearing," so too was our just and liberal society. With the same righteous fervor with which their predecessors ten years earlier had made the case for women, they made the case for children.

The rights of parents to self-expression and growth, which had been a primary concern in the '60s and '70s, were now said to be having adverse effects on the young. For every parent who could no longer live in a dead-end marriage, there was a child (or two) who had to cope with being a scion of divorce.

In the '70s, it was fashionable to believe that children did better if they were not part of an unhappy, tortured home, but that theory did not survive for long. Research by Judith Wallerstein, among others, confirmed what common sense dictated and wishful thinking did not—that children want and need two parents and do worse with only one. Early-'80s popular culture began to reflect this sobering idea; the overly hysterical *Shoot the Moon* portrayed a daughter devastated by the breakup of her parents and her father's subsequent guilty mania toward her.

For every mother who felt an obligation to herself and her gender to get out there in the work force, there was a child (or two) who came home from school to an afternoon of unsupervised indolence. Winn and Postman, both of whom are positively apocalyptic about the impact of television on the home, write of a nation of children riveted to the television screen, watching rock videos glorifying sex, cable movies glorifying violence, and television news inspiring so-called "copycat" crimes. The books most favored by little girls, Postman reports, are the novels of teen writers like Judy Blume and Norma Klein, who treat issues like masturbation and the loss of virginity with clinical matter-of-factness.

For many parents who enjoyed recreational drug use, there was a ten-year-old child whose observation of this behavior inevitably led to his own experimentation. One parent immortalized in Marie Winn's *Children without Childhood*, Dorothy Green, tells the story of her daughter, Betsy: "Betsy was thirteen, I guess, the summer she began to smoke dope with us. We always smoked openly at home, but we never let Betsy or her friends smoke at our house. But that summer we smoked a lot, and she'd be sitting there with us. . . . We felt closer to her that summer than we ever had. . . . I don't know when Betsy first started smoking dope. It was certainly long before that summer . . . I think we probably should have been much stricter about it. But we were feeling, 'Well, this is what we do, and why pretend? She knows we smoke.' " Finally, after Betsy turns to harder drugs and promiscuity, her parents are forced into action. "There we were, put in the role of old-fashioned, repressive parents. That's what was so bizarre. Because we're just the opposite, really. But somehow Betsy had to create in us that image, had to make us into oppressive parents. I kept saying, 'I'm being put in a role and I don't want to play it! I hate this role!' But I *had* to take on that role."*

---

* In her sickeningly fascinating book, Marie Winn exploits another noteworthy phenomenon of the '80s: people with no sense of shame who will say anything to journalists. Trend stories—the heart of American cultural journalism—could not be written today without the complete cooperation of a generation of extremely foolish baby boomers who think nothing of exposing their worst sides to writers who can hardly believe their dumb luck at

Winn and Postman expressed their concern for the well-being of America's children with the apocalyptic hyperbole typical of the decade's social philosophers. The threat of television to our young, Neil Postman said, was of a world-historical nature: "Just as phonetic literacy altered the predispositions of the mind in Athens in the fifth century B.C., just as the disappearance of social literacy in the fifth century A.D. helped create the medieval mind, just as typography enhanced the complexity of thought—indeed, changed the content of the mind—in the sixteenth century, then so does television make it unnecessary for us to distinguish between the child and the adult. For it is in its nature to homogenize mentalities."

Today, both books seem remarkably dated, in large measure because they were written prior to the explosion of the issue that would make the point about the way in which children were ill-used by adults: sexual abuse and incest.

Child abuse had first become a subject for general discussion during the '70s, at a time when the Women's Liberation movement made a systematic study of the ways in which men had brutalized and victimized women throughout the ages. The issue was part of a larger one, known as "domestic violence," and though it ended up on a couple of news magazine covers, it never really caught on as a major public concern.

But when sex with children replaced the battering of wives as the central focus of domestic crime, the issue became a mass phenomenon—with results comparable to the Salem witch trials.

---

getting such juicy quotes. *Newsweek* regularly relies on people who will tell its correspondents the most horrifying and narcissistic stories about themselves for its trend covers, those indelible articles with titles like "No Baby on Board" and "The Year of the Yuppie" and "The '80s Are Over: The Greed Decade Comes to an End." Inevitably, those who tell tales on themselves conclude their stories with phrases like, "I guess that makes me sound kind of awful, but that's just the way I am." Their arrival on the scene makes reading the society and cultural pages of our major newspapers and magazines more an act of voyeurism than ever before. All the same, it does indicate that this high level of self-obsession—self-obsession so profound that it has no room for shame or even dissimulation—is still with us.

It hit the public consciousness, after a few years of careful preparation, with the airing of a 1984 television movie about incest called *Something about Amelia*.

A phone number appeared at the end of the broadcast of *Something about Amelia*, as a voice offered counseling and support to those who might want to call in and talk about their own experiences with incest or child abuse. In the hours that followed, tens of thousands of people called in. Senator Paula Hawkins publicly confessed that she had been abused as a child. A highly publicized *Los Angeles Times* poll claimed subsequently that some 38 million Americans had been sexually abused in some way at some time by someone in their youth.

As soon as the sexual abuse of children became a matter of major public discussion, the legal system was rocked by a series of dramatic prosecutions. Seven employees of the McMartin day care center in California were charged (and subsequently acquitted) on 253 counts of abuse. In Jordan, Minnesota, seventy-five town residents were charged in what amounted to a town-wide case of molestation. A few years later, the upper middle class of New York City had its own incident to cope with when a lawyer named Joel Steinberg was arrested for the murder of his adopted six-year-old daughter, Lisa.

One might well have believed that the entire fabric of the society was unraveling in a way that even the most rabid opponent of that most bourgeois institution, the family, could hardly have imagined. But in truth the extent of the problem had been drastically and even viciously overstated—indeed, the *Los Angeles Times* poll was a preposterous overstatement, drawing inferences from political polling methods entirely inapplicable to sociological research. In the courts, the McMartin and Jordan cases crumbled into dust after years of investigation and millions of dollars in investigative expenses, not to say incalculable social and psychic cost to those who were publicly accused but never adequately tried (and never given a public acquittal) for their supposed crimes.

In addition, judges and legal reporters noted a drastic and troubling increase in the number of divorcing wives who accused their husbands of abusing their children. The evidence was slim but the accusation itself was, at least for a time, enough to deny a man all visitation rights to his children. Quickly enough, it became clear that child abuse was being used as yet another vindictive weapon in divorce proceedings, proving that the human desire for revenge, already theoretically infinite, had managed in the face of all reason to expand.

Whether the child-abuse problem has been overstated or not, the outbreak of public concern about the issue prompted a revision in the cultural image of children set only a few years before by Steven Spielberg. The abused children we watch in movies like *Something about Amelia* or are told about in news reports and in books like John Crewdson's *By Silence Betrayed: The Sexual Abuse of Children in America* seem very little like Elliott and his friends. They are not competent, do not seem adult, do not seem capable and in control of themselves. Rather, they appear helpless, the hapless prey of evil adults who are smarter and more sophisticated than they and can bribe, plead, cajole, or otherwise sweet-talk them into anything. Not only does it appear that family members can talk children into performing sexual acts; the problem with the McMartin and Jordan prosecutions was that *social workers* were talking children into *claiming* they had been sexually abused. The same pattern is true in divorce-inspired claims of incestuous abuse.

Grisly as all of this may sound, it was nonetheless a sign of health for the nation to have revised the view of children that dominated popular culture in the '70s. It was a further sign of health that the cultural infantilism of the early '80s passed even more quickly. The last thing children need (or want) to be told is that they are morally and intellectually superior to adults. What they want (and need) from adults is guidance and supervision—even from adults barely prepared to play that role. That the baby boomers had finally begun to grasp this basic fact was easily deduced from the return of actual, honest-to-God children and parents that began in 1984 with "The Cosby Show" and that was everywhere in evidence by the end of the decade. John Candy even spent an entire movie preserving his teenage niece's virginity in the amazingly reactionary *Uncle Buck*, made by John Hughes, one of the leaders of the kid-worship school earlier in the decade.

Unfortunately, the cultural pendulum now appears to be rapidly swinging toward the other extreme. Having once viewed their children as omnicompetent, the baby boomers now see them as possessed of an infinite capacity for victimization. No longer threatened by murderous and crippling diseases like polio, children are now prey (or so we think) to even more pernicious and crippling threats to their health, both physical and psychological. One aspirin too many leads to Reye's Syndrome. An Alar-coated apple a day? Don't ask. An HIV-positive child could bite your kid during recess. Her teacher might be molesting her in a secret dungeon under the day-care center. Your husband could be sneaking into her room. Drug dealers lurk on every corner, and their first target is *your child*.

Children, in short, have become a public-policy issue. In the eyes of the articulate class, the protection of children is so massive an undertaking as to require government intervention in every aspect of a child's life, from the radon in his bedroom to the school system that educates him badly to the unsafe streets on which he walks. To be sure, none of these threats is wholly imaginary. But a rational human being simply cannot deal collectively with children as an "issue." A rational human being can only deal with children one at a time, child by child by child. Treating children as a problem in public policy, by contrast, is precisely the kind of thing that makes parents feel powerless, incompetent, unable to deal with the immediate matters facing them. Just like Elliott's mother, in fact.

The baby boomers, it seems, are still looking for a way to shed the oppressive responsibilities of traditional parenthood.

Nothing has changed but the preferred escape route. Once the boomers confidently expected their competent children to look out for themselves; now, obsessed with an endless catalogue of potential horrors, they no less confidently expect the state to look out for them. This is, in nascent form, the newest pop culture assault on parenthood: the anxiety attack.

How I Got to Be Political

Dana Mack

I suppose I should already have begun to feel the crushing weight of history when in the fall of 1968 and at the age of fourteen I entered San Francisco's Lowell High School. My family, after all, had been been in Vienna when, a few months before school started, the Russians put an end to the prolonged and euphoric Prague spring. The Viennese wept openly in the streets, and our every encounter with them, however small, left us with the clear impression that America had somehow failed them.

I came from a suburban high school where, the year before, racial tensions had exploded into open violence. I had, in fact, been recruited onto what can only be described as a clean-up committee. The immediate cause of the riots was the problem of providing adequate transportation for black students who lived as far as five miles from school. This pressing issue having been settled, the committee went on to examine the widening chasm between black imputations and white culpability. It was a time of tremendous confusion and anger, and I remember thinking that it would be impossible to deal with all the grievances that were likely to emerge in our committee's discussions. At one conference, I was challenged by a black student five years older and about a foot taller than me to declare my willingness to marry a black man or admit myself a racist. At the age of thirteen, I hadn't thought much about the subject of marriage, but I answered, ingenuously enough, "If I loved him . . . and if he were Jewish."

1968 was also the year of the assassination of Robert Kennedy, and of the "police riot" at the Democratic Presidential convention in Chicago. In addition, it was the high-water mark of the hippie movement. All of these things added up to something less than cause for clear-eyed hope among the young. But hope was easy enough for me, a child hailed at home as a prodigy, schooled in the niceties of social occasions, and generally allowed the run of the refrigerator. And my first days at Lowell High were encouraging enough. At a time when neighboring Haight-Ashbury was its national focal point, the "tune in, turn on, drop out" crowd was noticeably absent from Lowell. "Hanging out," the accepted term for loitering in wait of adventure (and a great pastime at my former school), was generally discouraged. The biggest racial concern at Lowell involved the struggle of new Asian students to perfect their English. Even the school's lone bow to fashion, the institution of a "modular" scheduling system by which the administration abdicated all responsibility for the profitable use of student time, was greeted by a yawn and the inevitable sign-up for third-year math.

I worked hard at geometry; I was admitted into an advanced English class; I discovered the cafeteria-made peanut butter cookies which, if you came to school early enough, could be purchased (at twenty-five cents a shot) warm from the oven. Alas, only the cookies lived up to their promise. Those cookies, in fact, turned out to be the best thing about Lowell High School. In the darkest days of my adolescence, they provided me with my only good reason to get out of the bed and go to school.

How to explain the doldrums into which I sank? There was, to begin with, my English teacher, Mrs. Y. Despite her liver-spotted hands and spinsterly sartorial habits, Mrs. Y had young ideas. Her sole object in introducing literature to tender young bourgeois minds was to permeate them with the overriding notion of decay. Not for her were Shakespeare's rhetoric, or Jane Austen's wit. Not for her were patriotic speeches, or praise of connubial love. The love she extolled in class was that of J. Alfred Prufrock; her native country was *The Waste Land*. With her, we read the plays of Tennessee Williams and Eugene O'Neill. We learned of birth in Dublin and death in Venice. It struck me at the time that her main criterion for the selection of literature suitable for classroom use was its power to depress.

I owe to Mrs. Y the first self-doubts of my adolescence. It was a foggy winter afternoon, and I approached her with the request (a naive one, it turned out) to accompany a group of classmates to an Andrew Wyeth exhibition. She raised an eyebrow and smiled an impenetrably compassionate smile. "I am afraid," she said in the bare whisper that was her trademark, "that the museum tours are for the *special* students." (The word "special" had not yet come to mean "handicapped" in Mrs. Y's carefully cultivated tongue.)

I asked *exactly* what that meant.

"Well," she said, unabashed, "students in the upper two percent."

"I—I'm not exactly a stranger to art, Mrs. Y," I protested inanely. "Actually, I study piano."

"Yes," she replied unflinchingly, and smiled her compassionate smile. "I'm so sorry."

Most of the other students in Mrs. Y's English class were in the "upper two," and I always felt that they, along with Mrs. Y, barely tolerated my presence, the result of what she described as my "flowering in the area of writing." It didn't help matters any that I chose to talk at length in class about books that I quite obviously lacked the moral strength to have read clear through to the end, or that I constantly related all of these half-read masterpieces to the struggles of the Jewish people. This last tendency sometimes led to embarrassing situations, for many of my classmates were products of mixed marriages in which (despite the conspicuous family names) the Jewish partner was ambivalent about his heritage.

But far more separated me from my classmates than the simple fact that they took college math and chemistry, and stayed as far away as possible from modern Hebrew. I showed off in class; they were careful never to exhibit any personal vanity. It was as unimportant for them to actively seek visibility as it was for them to wash their hair regularly. And why should it have been important? They were the standard by which all things were measured; as long as they came in on Mrs. Y's downbeat, there was nothing more to prove. It was hurtful to me that they refused to greet me in the halls, but I made up my mind early to seek my friends elsewhere. And I did not fail to notice the peculiar irony of their snobbery, an irony rooted in the fact that they constituted the core of the left at Lowell High.

Their politics didn't matter to me, not at first. But being an outsider encouraged me to take a closer look at their taste, which even then struck me as humorless and provincial. I remember a particularly appalling afternoon of recitations from *Spoon River Anthology*, accompanied by Erik Satie's *Trois Gymnopédies* as arranged for guitar and recorder. I also remember the day I got myself selected for the drama department's performance of a postmodernist effort by Jean-Claude van Itallie. I wanted it badly. I think that what attracted me to this play was the poker-faced line "Blah, blah, blah, penis." It seemed to me a pithy and accurate paraphrase of our daily discussions in English class. I had the good luck to speak this line on stage, in the character of an old lady. It was the lone coup of my high school career.

Like most adolescents, I often felt lonely and unappreciated. More to the point, I felt that the weave of my soul was fraying from constant pulling in so many directions. My natural social milieu should have been that of the smartly dressed, upper-middle-class Jewish girls of Lowell High, an apolitical assortment of budding JAPS (the movement to ban that acronym as being insufficiently sensitive not yet having gotten underway) bound for marriage to what would someday be called "yuppies." Had I been cast more in the "junior petite" mold, had I been of less intellectual bent, had I been less in love with Vladimir Ashkenazy (who seemed to me at that point in my life to be the very embodiment of the music of Chopin), I might have made it into this circle.

I wanted desperately to go to their parties, though I couldn't imagine what I would talk about when I got there. Twice I even received invitations. The parties were given "out," in the rented facilities of hotels and private clubs. They involved nothing more insidious than the obtuse aping of outmoded conventions. Here, girls met boys over the punch bowl, though what they did after the party seemed not to be the object of any particular parental concern. (My date for one of these parties took it upon himself to rent a motel room on Lombard Street, his stated object being "to get down to some serious drinking." Not being a serious drinker, it took me only ten minutes to bore him.) I could have had a party of my own at a club. My parents offered to throw one. But I hated rock music—and I was secretly afraid that nobody would come.

As it turned out, my best friends were all free-spinning atoms who had in common only an unusually severe attachment to novels. One of them, a girl who bore a distinguished Italian name, had a great passion for South American writers and a weakness for marijuana. We occasionally smoked together in (of all places!) the ladies' room of the Stonestown Macy's. I also spent quite a bit of time with a group of girls whose parents were Jewish refugees from Germany via Israel. I found their religious conservatism and modesty congenial. What I remember best about them, though, was that we giggled a lot together, and endlessly planned Lucullan feasts. On the occasions of these feasts, I talked with their parents about Beethoven and the fortunes of the local opera season. I had mixed feelings when I visited their simple homes. I was embarrassed by the comparative opulence of my parents' house; I was amazed by the fact that these uprooted people could be of such good cheer (I was a fourth-generation San Franciscan); I envied their intellectual confidence. In their presence I felt for the first time the all-embracing authority of Goethe and Schiller for Germans—a burden which, I think, oppressed these Germans even as it sustained them.

I wish I could say that I discovered myself politically under their straitlaced influence. But I didn't. Instead, I tried on the left for size. It was the most obvious choice, but it didn't fit.

I remember a day in the spring of 1970, the day before the Moratorium. I danced and chanted "Out now!" in the front corridor of Lowell High for a good five minutes. It left me numb with chagrin.

Not long before, I had accompanied the son of a friend of my mother on a day trip to Disneyland. The trip was a gift from my parents to a young man about to be shipped out to Vietnam and already far from his fragile home in Florida. We rode the rides and ate the plastic-tasting ice cream; we said little to each other. When we returned home, David asked me to go with him to Fillmore West that evening. To my utter dismay, my parents encouraged me to go. The Grateful Dead must have been playing that night, because I remember thinking in the middle of all that noise that I would be grateful to be dead.

After the concert, David and I came home and sat up late into the night, looking out the window at the Golden Gate Bridge. I smoked every one of the cigarettes from the pack of Salems I had stolen from our living-room end table. For a long time we sat quietly in the clouds of smoke. Then he said, "You sort of wonder whether you're coming back." At that moment, I thought that all wars might be as senseless as they are inevitable. But I didn't pursue the idea. Instead, I thanked my lucky stars that I was a girl.

I thought of my evening with David on the day before the

Moratorium. I remembered his numb farewells to us, and I remembered the old wide-brimmed purple hat that he insisted on leaving with us. He said he would reclaim it when he returned. I wondered whether anyone or anything on his last day in America had given him a reason for going to Vietnam. I wondered if anyone or anything had given him a reason to want to come home.

On the morning of the Moratorium, I read a column in the *San Francisco Chronicle* suggesting that a sudden withdrawal of American troops from Southeast Asia would result in a bloodbath in Vietnam and Cambodia. I clipped the column and took it with me to school. After announcements detailing the day's activities, which included the cutting of classes and the wearing of black armbands, I asked my homeroom teacher for permission to read the editorial aloud. I walked to the podium. My recitation was received with stunned silence. I was committed.

Oddly, nothing much changed for me at Lowell High School after that. Though some of the ROTC men now recognized and greeted me, I was still friendly with the same voracious bookworms and the same giggling German-Israeli girls. I still smoked dope from time to time in the ladies' room of the Stonestown Macy's. I remained uninvited to the parties of the affluent Jews. My academic record, especially in English, remained unremarkable. I continued to dream of dinner with Vladimir Ashkenazy, a dinner which my mother finally wangled through the good offices of an impresario friend of ours. (I spent an hour and a half putting on false eyelashes for the occasion.) But one thing was different: I was a conservative.

Only one of my classmates said anything even remotely disparaging about my new political affiliation, and he said it after we left school. One summer day after my freshman year at college, I met one of the half-Jews who had gone off to Harvard.

We were in a supermarket aisle too small for us to pretend not to have noticed each other. "Hey," he called out, "where did you end up?"

"At Berkeley."

"Oh, yeah?" He looked amused. (Berkeley had never been much respected by the Harvard crowd.) "Well, don't tell me *you've* become a radical!"

"I didn't go to university to learn politics," I snapped back, surprised at my confidence. But it was the simple truth. Politics, after all, was about the only thing I had learned at Lowell High.

A Whiff of Grapeshot

Lisa Schiffren

*I*n the fall of 1987, two young men I knew, a Democratic government official and a Republican party leader, were planning their first runs for elected office in the Midwestern state where I covered politics. Here, I thought, was the voice of the New Generation: they were young, articulate, intelligent, Ivy League-educated baby boomers. Both of my friends were convincing in defense of their very different political convictions. They both had solid experience. Each had a sense of humor. They were good guys, the best their parties had to offer. They looked good. They spoke well. They even thought substantively.

So why did I come away from interviewing them with the feeling that something intangible was missing? Why did they ultimately seem insubstantial?

Politics is talk, image, theater, all to a much larger degree than most other professions. But proving yourself by winning a debate over policy or strategy is a self-referential credential, nothing more. It means little in the wide world beyond the political arena, the real world upon which politicians act. Statecraft demands more than just political experience. Neither of these likable young men had ever been tested by fire. How could I gauge whether there was steel at their cores, whether they could lead or merely negotiate, act or only debate?

Their generation—my generation—has been raised in a culture of words, a culture in which being articulate is counted the greatest public asset a leader can have and in which choosing between verbal constructs and political models is how people arrive at principles. A purely verbal culture is easily divorced from reality. Our civilization's hard-tested understanding of human nature has been talked away by those who offer utopian notions subject only to the tests of rhetoric: Does the speech, the sound, bite, the story have a plausible internal logic? And is the message attractive enough to sell?

"In politics," a thirty-year-old Afghan guerrilla leader who had been fighting for a decade recently told me, "everything is a trick. In the war, if you face a Soviet you kill him, or he kills you." Combat tests mettle; the LSATs do not. War hones decisiveness, determination, and a sense of responsibility for one's actions in a way that hustling on a commodities trading floor does not. In years to come, nations like Afghanistan will have plenty of eager young men, refined and proven in the forge of war, fit to shoulder responsibility for leading their societies. What about us?

In the second half of the baby boom are many much-educated men and women, ambitious for power. But for the first time in our history, we face a shortage of people whose characters have been shaped by decisive action, by the irreducible tests of bravery and discipline that Americans routinely faced in wars or on the frontier for most of our history through the '50s. Until our time, the American culture understood such tests as critical to its nature, even celebrated them as part of its self-image. In those days, "rugged" described much of life in much of our country; it wasn't just an adjective used to sell footwear and cars meant for weekend play.

The older baby boomers (those born between 1946 and 1955) were barely touched by that culture, which ended with the unprecedented affluence that followed World War II. Facing Vietnam, they rejected the test, then justified their rejection convincingly enough to sway the society itself—or at least its public voices in media and government—to their way of thinking. But not content with escaping service, or even with opposing a specific war for specific reasons, the baby boom's educated elites took the extra step of devising a tortured moral protest against the very rationale for war itself.

Even more insidiously for the long run, the baby boom intellectuals effectively deconstructed the normal mythologizing processes that accompany any war. Stories of exemplary heroism and valor, sometimes embellished, often stylized, confirm the importance of these virtues to society and inspire more such action. Though this process is a spontaneous one, it also turns out to be quite fragile. The practical effect of subjecting this internal cultural support to hostile, unappeasable scrutiny was a stunning devaluation of traditional notions of duty, discipline, valor, honor, self-sacrifice, intrepidity, contempt of softness, respect, glory. . . .

In short, the military virtues and values—which, though rarely central to American culture, held honored positions as buttresses to freedom—were found by the older baby boomers not to be virtues at all. Discipline was reduced to authoritarianism; duty interfered with the higher calling of self-fulfillment; obedience was slavish submission to authority, which should be questioned at every juncture; the quest for glory was mere adventurism. Honor was found to be entirely a charade, unwinnable in any forum that involved defending the morally indefensible principles on which our culture rests. This demonizing of war and things martial still reaches such absurd extremes that politically correct boomer moms are reluctant to let their little boys play with toy guns and soldiers. Last year, convulsed by fear that it was sending the wrong message, the Methodist Church actually attempted to change the words of its signature hymn, "Onward, Christian Soldiers."

So we don't have many public heroes among our thousands of Vietnam veterans. Not that there wasn't a normal distribution of heroism or honor or bravery. It's just that it wasn't publicly recognized in the dirty political fight over the war. In fact, relatively few heroes emerged in any public sphere during the '60s and '70s. A hero, after all, is larger than life. Heroism conflicted with the boomer elite's vision of a morally contaminated society to admit that people can rise above the compromises daily life demands, to take meaningful action within the parameters of traditional society.

In any case, the bitter rift among the boomers is unlikely to ever fully heal, as the fracas over Dan Quayle's wartime behavior and the media psychoanalyzing that attempted to explain Oliver North's Contra policy as a reaction to his experience in Vietnam both suggest. Their definitions of political good are permanently divided. Though a few politicians have emerged from the ranks of the Vietnam vets, it's hard to imagine that hordes of leaders are waiting in the wings. Actually, it's a relief to know that, having become disillusioned with politics, the older boomers are immersing themselves in private life. They've done quite enough already, thanks.

I was a sophomore in high school when Saigon fell. The antiwar movement was a looming, often intrusive, but imperfectly comprehended backdrop to my childhood. All my junior high school friends were vaguely political, and being "antiwar" was politically correct. But since the war (that is, the draft) never threatened us personally, it was all very diluted.

It's not surprising that the younger boomers, those who came of age after Vietnam, have less of an irrational antipathy to the use of force. Of those who cared to look, many of us were struck by the consequences of valuing "peace" (or, to be more precise, noninvolvement) too highly in a world where great powers can't always pick their fights. Some of us came to this conclusion when we noticed that Israel's defense needs, for instance, were not the fabrication of the wily "military-industrial complex." After Vietnam came Cambodia, Angola, Nicaragua, Afghanistan, where innocents were slaughtered by uninvited might. And retreat did not win us friends among our allies. So we voted for Ronald Reagan, for increased defense spending, for facing down the Soviets and their proxies, in numbers that shocked and horrified our older siblings.

The late '80s saw a gradual backing away from the hyper-moralism that previously colored elite opinion about warfare, whether in defense of U.S. interests or on behalf of an ally. Popular support for the use of force has made something of a comeback, though in a highly qualified, rarely exercised form, unlikely to admit of much use. Panama, the operation that closed the '80s, is the perfect illustration of the kind of military action that is now permissible. It was very brief; the Bush administration worried in public that it would lose domestic support if it dragged on more than a few weeks. It had the highly specific goal of toppling a nasty small-time dictator whose main threat to the U.S. was terminal embarrassment of the administration. Manuel Noriega, who had been thoroughly demonized beforehand, had no support here at home, as other more ruthless Moscow-backed dictators in our hemisphere have had. There was plenty of flag-waving, and few American deaths. All told, the action went smoothly enough to be considered a smashing success during the brief moments it registered on the media screen, which marks a real turnaround.

At the same time, though, our society's daily life is more wholly divorced from things military than it ever has been before. This long-term trend has been given further momentum by the revelation, in the fall of 1989 and winter of 1990, that we have won the Cold War. There are those who like to claim that the Reagan military buildup and the President's hard-line "cowboy" image did much to turn the tide from defeatism and the infamous Carterite "malaise." This effect was especially profound among the clients and allies who look to the U.S. as the guarantor of their liberties. They argue that this display of hardware and bravado catalyzed the ongoing Soviet implosion. As important as arms and steadfast resolution were, I think we owe our victory to a different strength. We have won the ideological war of our times, or the Communists have lost it, to an astonishing extent because of our stockpiles of VCRs and soft toilet paper. We won because we have miniskirts, Walkmen, and Big Macs—and because everyone else wants them. We certainly did not impress the world with our Spartan prowess, discipline, and determination. It wasn't our MX missile-basing plan, or the Star Wars defensive shield we haven't built, or the ferocious will to power of our Congressmen, that intimidated the Soviets. Rather, we have displayed our vast wealth and showed how natural the getting of it can be, creating a worldwide desire to emulate our ways rather than the Soviets'.

The effect cannot be gainsaid. Yet here at home, little has changed. We are softer, sleeker, and more self-satisfied (and indulgently self-critical) than ever. Our economy continues to boom, but our culture continues to decline. We have learned no hard lessons. We have won the Cold War without regaining the virtues a nation needs to win a hot one. Indeed, we are now striving mightily to convince ourselves that there will never be another big war.

War in America has become a policy metaphor, used when politicians wish to convey tough action and a hard reckoning with reality. Of course in politics the reckoning rarely comes, nor do "wars" on social ills—drugs, sexually transmitted diseases, illiteracy—elicit sacrifice or the decisive action of combat. Lacking any correlative in our society, the metaphor of war is truly dead language. In fact, we are more likely to pursue real war and military action in the feckless, desultory manner long reserved for domestic policy. Our detachment leaves us increasingly unable to believe that others are wholly engaged, that they lust for power in their blood and will shed others' blood to grasp it. For men like Saddam Hussein, words are toys they send skidding across a floor. We scramble to calibrate their vectors and velocity as if they were real, when for them only action is real. Similarly, we read the Middle East as if it were the Midwest, fighting over negotiable, divisible commodities instead of the fundamental terms of national existence. And even as we watched the people of Romania or the students in China shedding their blood in the street confrontations that meant enough to elicit such sacrifice, the lasting policy debate that emerged from our own venture in Panama was not "What price freedom?" but whether, on the strength of a captured dog kennel, women should serve in combat.

This distance is partly an inevitable consequence of our long-running current peace, partly due to the deep and lasting influences of the "peace movement," whether in its anti-Vietnam or anti-nuke phases, and partly a result of longer-term cultural trends.

"War is the continuation of state policies by other means," Clausewitz wrote famously some two hundred years ago in *On War*. War, in the Napoleonic era that Clausewitz described, was an integral part of the range of legitimate responses a state might offer to a given political situation, though its consequences were perfectly well understood to be more drastic than some other alternatives. In our time this is no longer true. Today war is not placed on a continuum with other political action. On the contrary, it is seen as a discontinuity, the antithesis of political activity. Not merely an extreme response or a costly tool of policy, war is viewed as a sign that the entire political system has failed. Avoiding war and maintaining an ever cozier peace is generally understood to be the whole point of international politics.

We have mirrored this political notion by revising war out of history. War, which until two decades ago was the backbone of the discipline's structure, has been relegated to the sidelines (or the academic backwater of military history), supplanted by the various social histories which study daily life under what is considered the more ordinary circumstance of peace. Similarly, the pervasive impression is that defense spending is an unnatural appendage to the economy, a monkey carried on its back, which at best distorts an economy's priorities and at worst is ruinous. Forget that it may undergird our stability. War now is generally understood as an aberrational condition which, like a disease, only weakens a society.

The diminishing threat of warfare among the liberal democracies seems to suggest that humanity has evolved politically. But economics, not politics, deserves the credit. The decline of the heroic values owes much to the centuries-long rise of bourgeois culture. Traditional European armies, peopled by officers from the rural gentry and peasant infantries, were natural antagonists of the productive urban traders and proprietors who were excluded from the military and scorned by it, and who in turn scorned its aristocratic, nonproductive ways. In principle and in practice, the ideals of chivalric honor, glory, and bravery stand in opposition to the less romantic, more practical activities of commerce and the prosperity it engenders—activities that flourish best under conditions of peace and stability, without the inevitable high taxes of wartime.

Through the end of the nineteenth century, it was presumed in the U.S. that the two traditions could live in a steady tension, keeping us both rich and fit, comfortable and free. But where war breeds a desire for peace, affluence merely stimulates the desire for expanding comfort. With the closing of the frontiers and the simultaneous rise of all manner of specious social movements, American leaders were moved to fear for the spiritual resilience of the Republic should the specter of eternal peace and progress, socialism, feminism, and vegetarianism triumph. Teddy Roosevelt (no champion of any of the above-mentioned causes) vehemently admonished that we not become a nation of "mollycoddles" and "weaklings," overvaluing wealth at the expense of honor and strength.

William James, the Harvard philosopher who was a pacifist and a socialist, exemplified the worry in his well-known essay "The Moral Equivalence of War." James began by mocking those who believe that only war will preserve us from degenerating into "a world of clerks and teachers, of co-education and zo-ophily, of 'consumer's leagues' and 'associated charities,' of in-dustrialism unlimited and feminism unabashed. No scorn, no hardness, no valor any more! Fie upon such a cattleyard of a planet!" But he quickly backed down, suggesting that in moder-ation this is a healthy sentiment: "Militarism is our great pres-erver of our ideals of hardihood, and human life with no use for hardihood would be contemptible. Without risks or prizes for the darer, history would be insipid indeed."

We come late to the bloodiest, most contentious century our planet has known. After two world wars that left tens of millions dead, in an age of nuclear weaponry where massive, inglorious annihilation is a distantly hovering possibility, it's impossible to see war innocently. For us, it could never be the same exhilarat-ing crest of energies, the challenging ritual of manhood or the chivalric stand of civilization against the barbarians that it was a century ago, when Teddy Roosevelt charged up San Juan Hill and Winston Churchill joined the British Raj's Frontier Scouts, putting down rebellious tribes on the Empire's border. Imperi-alism is morally discredited. (Besides, who wants the burden of taking care of the conquered?) We rightly regard only defensive wars or punitive police actions as just and moral. So for anyone to suggest at all seriously that we will miss war, that we already do, that it has social utility beyond the Malthusian winnowing claims, invites charges of cynicism and worse.

Yet there is no getting away from the feeling that humanity's pugnacity must have its outlets; that unless discipline and hardi-ness are occasionally tested, their force dribbles away; that life and history without great passions worth fighting for—and the fights themselves—are a bleak and empty prospect. Life without real and hard tests is less than fully human. Life on the sidelines comes quickly to resemble images on a screen that we watch, absorbed, but without the smells and sounds, feelings or stakes, fast-running blood and sweat of engagement.

In his Vietnam novel *Fields of Fire*, James Webb depicts ambivalent, often disgusted soldiers fighting under conditions that preclude romanticism. Despite the pervasive and, one suspects, accurately rendered antiheroic sensibility of the soldiers, one antisocial street tough uses words to describe his experience that include: urgency, authority, fullness, life lived at full throttle. "He sensed," Webb writes, "that it was all here, everything. . . . All of life's compelling throbs, condensed and honed each time a bullet flew: the pain, the brother-love, the sacrifice. Nobility discovered by those who'd never even contemplated sacrifice, never felt an emotion worth their own blood on someone else's altar. The heartrending deaths. The successes. All here. None there, back in the bowels of the World. Except for the pain, and even that a numbed, daily pain, steady, like blue funk, not the sharp pain of an agonizing moment, capable of being purged, vindicated. . . ."

How will we replicate these peak experiences in our safe consumer culture? As the world embraces our consumption-driven view of the good life, as all corners of the globe are linked by the fax machines and modems that are the crown jewels of our consumer culture, how will we maintain frontiers, with their beckoning challenges? What place will be remote enough to avoid the pacifying, denaturing influences of our culture?

In war, nothing is more common than death. Paradoxically, this seems to teach a healthy respect for life. In our society, where death is kept at several removes, we have slipped over the line from respect to unconditional reverence for life (not all life, only our own lives) as we have sapped it of meaning. This has inflated its worth in our eyes as it has made death the object of neurotic, obsessive fear. So we exercise feverishly, eat noxious concoctions of sawdustlike grain hulks, and parcel out life's innocent indulgences in mean measures as if the sheer prospect of pleasure itself might harden our arteries and keep us from additional years of bran and mineral water. We seem to think that we can inoculate ourselves against death by spreading it thinly over most of our lives. Our inordinate fear of death takes its toll by diminishing our lives. It has left us with little tolerance for the pain, from personal failure to abstract social inequality, that is inescapably part of human life. We live in equal fear of pleasure. We even ask our government to make personal risks illegal.

A society that believes that life is worth little unless it is lived honorably has a better shot at keeping things in perspective. Honor, sometimes called the "divine folly," posits a moral rigor toward God, family, nation, and duty itself that we, with our fluid meanings and deconstructed morals, think mad. There is no rational explanation for one who values honor enough not to want to live without it, but this "fine contempt for life" yields more grace than those who cling to survival bring to life or death. Without such a fine contempt for life we can neither live well nor die well. It is one of the ironies of this society obsessed with death that we seem to have forgotten that a good life requires a good death.

In war, planning, strategy, all manner of thought are necessary, but war is decided in actions. Bravery—not rashness or foolhardiness, but solid physical courage—is the virtue action calls forth. In our culture, so dependent on words and images that are easily manipulated, things are seldom what they seem. It is one of the great attractions of the battlefield that victory can be measured and wins and losses tallied, just as it is obvious under fire who is brave and who is a coward, and why being brave is more virtuous than being a coward. When words are overvalued, the world finds itself hostage to ideologies that promise much but offer no proof that they can deliver—and hostage as well to clever men who seek to persuade without having to walk first into a hail of fire.

One night in the spring of 1987, I sat with several Afghan *mujahideen* in a mud-walled room of a remote valley clinic. Their tired, bearded faces were lighted by the orange glow of a kerosene lamp. The commander, a former teacher, tuned his short-wave radio to the BBC's Farsi newscast, which contained a lengthy report on the day's Iran-Contra hearings. I was more than a little puzzled at how closely these guerrillas followed the fortunes of gray background men like Richard Secord. But then it became clear.

"This scandal will not cause the President to fall, yes?" one man asked.

No, I didn't think so.

"There is an election next year, no? Do you think the President's party will win?" asked a voice loaded with concern. (They all knew where their Stinger missiles came from.)

"Who would you like to see win?"

"We hear that the Vice-President is a good man, a strong anti-Communist. Maybe even stronger anti-Communist than Reagan," the commander said.

Startled, I asked why he thought that about the mild-mannered George Bush.

"He was a big commander in your second war, and he ran the CIA. For us, someone strong like this is good," he said with certainty.

Back in Michigan, the setting was less exotic, but the answers were surprisingly similar. In high school gyms, I grabbed spectators at pre-primary rallies of the Republican faithful, a disproportionately conservative group, to ask who they were really going to vote for. Time and again the answer came back: "Bush."

"Why?"

"We need a strong leader."

"What makes you think he's a strong leader?"

"He was a war hero."

I noted the pattern but didn't quite get it. I respected Bush's actions as a brash young World War II pilot barely shot down before he was up and flying again. But to me politics was policy, and policy was ideas, and I didn't much see what having flown fighter planes had to do with those. Happily for President Bush, his campaign understood what the policy intellectuals who kept shouting for more details on arms control and monetary policy did not: in a Presidential race, leadership is the voting issue. And it is a universal presumption that war heroes—men who have displayed valor and selflessness—are fit to lead other men and nations.

Citizens are reassured by such records because we know that politicians in a democracy are inclined to sway with the shifting winds of social fashion. Passing the ultimate, irreducible test of bravery under fire is one of the few yardsticks we have to take a man's inner measure. Happily for America, we have had no shortage of these men, some of whom have acquired intellectual force to match their bravery.

Heroes make natural leaders. A good leader, military or civilian, maintains what military historian John Keegan calls a "mask of command." The authority of command is lost the second that psychologizing is allowed to replace action with critique of action. Dwelling on motive and excessive explanation of actions is a guarantee of diluted leadership. It won't work in situations where the obvious dangers call for reassuring certitude and the sense, even if it is an illusion, that someone is in control. And a leader who cannot maintain an iron mask in face of doubts, anxieties, and inevitable losses will not find other men following him.

To be intellectually sophisticated in our society means accepting to a greater or lesser degree that all meaning is subjective. When there is no ultimate reality to any fact, it is difficult to ascribe hierarchical virtues to actions.

Truth, it is said, is the first casualty of war. In fact, the opposite is truer; the rigorous, unflinching, unpoliticized assessment of facts on the ground is most necessary in wartime. In war it is just not possible to deconstruct the "facts on the ground," to distort them, or even to romanticize them, without tremendous cost. This was brought home to me starkly on the eve of an assault on several strategic posts at the edge of an Afghan city.

I had been traveling with a young guerrilla commander considered something of a rising star by his party's military office, which had given him a lot of scarce heavy weaponry and Stinger missiles. He was the designated commander for Jalalabad's western quadrant in the post-Soviet withdrawal attempt to take the city. Also present was an Afghan general, a tough, professional old soldier, there to evaluate the performance of the younger man who had so dazzled the desk jockeys back in Pakistan.

After days of watching the young commander make plans and deploy his men and artillery, the general offered me some advice. "A journalist is like a general," he said. "You must watch him [the commander] very closely and see only what he does and how well it works. You cannot afford to make him a hero just because you spent so much time with him and you want to write a story about a hero. You will look too stupid if you are wrong, just like my party will be stupid if we make him a big commander and he cannot fight."

Sadly for my profession, the general was wrong. Journalists, like politicians, are rarely accountable for their incorrect assessments or the liberties they take describing reality. But a general who wants to win cannot afford the delightful fantasies and attractive formulas we sell. He can afford nothing but cold, unclouded vision, or he risks wasting lives, position, and scarce materiel. It's a discipline our society, which regularly substitutes wishful thinking for reality, could use more of.

So it is worth wondering what will happen if war comes to us—and it's hard to imagine that it won't, sooner or later. What happens to a society so far from nature and human nature that its men do not know how to use guns or kill, and have little concrete, rooted idea of what they are defending?

There are a few hopeful signs. While the early boomers made a faith out of being antiwar, the later boomers have the advantage of agnosticism on the issue. Similarily, the early boomers must cling to their hard-won repudiation of meaning, because it cost them so much personally in normal satisfactions and mundane happiness. But the later boomers, having grown up on constantly shifting ground, schooled in insecurity and impermanence, seek traditional codes to live by. This desire tells in the churches, at the altar, and in GOP vote tallies whenever the question of defense and national strength is an issue.

I suspect we would rise to a real threat. I'd guess that many of us would eagerly leave our fast-track careers and insulated lives for the chance of a real test, given half an excuse. In fact, the dirty secret of my generation is a resurgent fascination with guns and war—in books, in movies, in video games. Yuppies stalk each other with dart guns and amuse themselves with the novels of Tom Clancy as if the peace movement of the '60's had never happened. Who doubts that they would find the real thing no less seductive?

Oliver Wendell Holmes, Jr., nobody's idea of a redneck, had much to say about the virtues of combat experience. He knew that it was "horrible and dull," but he knew that there was more to it than that. "High and dangerous action," he wrote, "teaches us to believe as right beyond dispute things for which our doubting minds are slow to find words of proof. Out of heroism grows faith in the worth of heroism."

For a generation with no heroes, a little heroism would be a fine thing to have around.

Portrait of a Washington Policy Wonk

David Brooks

A really top Washington policy wonk will get two invitations to a black-tie dinner given by—well, let's call it the Council on Responsible Priorities. He will get one sent to him at the office —Department of Commerce, Office of the Deputy Secretary (Legislative Liaison)—and one sent to his home, owing to the fact that he was a CRP fellow for a few years prior to his appointment. If he accepts the latter invitation, he will get seated next to some young journalists and a few fellow wonks. The journalists will dominate the conversation with that imperial manner of theirs, and the conversation will be about whatever that day's issue-blip happens to be: the budget talks, a resignation, an oil leak. Journalists get opinions the way most people get the flu; if one is going around, they catch it.

If, on the other hand, the wonk accepts the invitation afforded him because of his job—his awesome power—he will get placed next to one of those uncouth dolts from Dayton, Ohio, who donate the money to support these dinners. In that case, the conversation will be mostly about commuting times. The dolt will also talk a lot about the current state of the tool business. He will be accompanied by a quiet, homely wife, trying to hold up her end of being in a room with the President of the United States and all those Senators. She'll look astonished, though not half so astonished as she is over the fact that the man she married, who used to wheel movie projectors around to classrooms in high school, ended up with more wealth than Croesus.

The choice is an easy one. The wonk accepts the invitation aforded him by virtue of his job. The conversation will be inane, but he will be stroked like crazy by this overawed couple. He'll imagine the dolt going back to the country club in Dayton and clumsily dropping his name: "Well, I had dinner with the Deputy Secretary of Commerce in Washington the other day, a good friend of mine named Frank Richards, and he assured me that the Fed . . ." Such are the conversations that wonk orgasms are made of.

The wonk arrives at the dinner too late for the crush of cocktails, just as people are being seated in the hotel ballroom. Guests are pecking around amidst the numbered tables, then dashing from dinner place to dinner place, growing more desperate as they come across everybody's dinner card but their own. The bottles of unremarkable white wine have already been allocated sparsely among the settings. The corpulent, middle-aged waiters are bowling over the guests in the manner of buffalo stampeding through gnats. The plates, which have done service since the legendary CIO conventions of the '50s, are invariably bunched toward one side of the table. As the diners sit down, each wonders if the water glass on his right or his left is his. Inevitably the wonk's neighbors each take the glasses adjacent to his plate, and it is not until mid-meal that he will notice that the only free glass is on the other side of the centerpiece and miles out of reach. Ditto the dinner roll.

In lieu of conversation, everybody picks up the evening program and spends the next twenty minutes or so poring over the list of attendees, checking his own name first and then noting satisfactorily the galaxy of big names who are sharing in this gathering. Some of the names are extraordinarily big, and from both sides of the aisle. The CRP is a centrist think tank (wonks don't hang with yahoos), and of course our hero wonk is firmly moderate in his views. The whole point of being a moderate is that it doubles the field of possible dinner guests.

Glancing around the ballroom, one sees the unmoneyed aristocracy of Washington gathered in all its splendid blandness. These are the cautious careerist Anglo-Saxons who switch on "Meet the Press" on Sunday mornings for background noise as they do their vacuuming. Let us be clear: these people do their own cleaning. They do not live along Foxhall Road or attend the upper-upper dinner parties at the embassies, nor do they get written up in *Regardie's*. This set is one step down the ladder. They live in McLean with addresses like 37 Terrace Circle Court if they are Republican and in Chevy Chase if they are Democrats. They have a combined family income of between $70,000 and $150,000 (all Democratic families have two incomes; most of the Republicans do as well). They are more concerned with issues than the society set. They work for think tanks in the administration or on the Hill, or they once did—some have cashed in and joined law firms or lobbying outfits. (The most shameless have become flacks.) They write for op-ed pages and policy magazines. They think they could outwit Buchanan if they could only get on McLaughlin. Often enough they are asked to sit on panels in front of C-Span cameras (their insomniac cousin in Nevada invariably calls the next day to congratulate them). Once a year they get an invite from "MacNeil/Lehrer." Divided from the elite by money and class, they are divided from the ideologues by temperament. They are not alienated, nor do they hold irresponsible views. Most of the men were treasurers at the second-best fraternities on the campuses of Midwestern state universities.

The wonk dresses well and unobtrusively (only right-wingers wear unnatural fibers). His suit deemphasizes his shoulders, just as the women at this dinner wear dresses to deemphasize their breasts and legs (pornographers would find nothing of professional interest here). The wonk is good-looking, with his sandy brown hair and wire-rimmed glasses, but he is not *too* good-looking. Nobody is especially beautiful at these dinners. All the rewards for beauty are in New York or Los Angeles; in Washington it would breed doubts about your soundness. The wonk glances around the room and is comfortable with the fact that living in Washington means never having to change your hair style.

His dinner companions exactly meet his expectations. There is indeed the rube contributor (as it turns out, he builds propellers). His wife sits at his side. The rest of the table is filled by men who, while quite famous, are also known for their dreary conversational styles. On the other side of the rube's wife sits a professor of some sort who in some long-forgotten epoch established a reputation for being a deep thinker. He quotes from *The Federalist Papers* as much as possible. On the other side of him is a middle-aged journalist who is a leading member of Washington's Club of the Gravely Concerned. Last week, he had his brow furrowed over the twin deficits. The week before, he was worrying about the way television sound bites make it impossible for the nation to develop an informed electorate. Today he is concerned about encroachments on the First Amendment. (This re-proves the theory that journalists who worry about the First Amendment are so unfailingly tedious that they could not conceivably put together a sentence that anybody of any persuasion could conceivably want to censor.) Next to him is the good journalist's wife, an activist of some sort who comes to all these dinners and talks about nothing but her efforts to empower the people who are not invited. The one with his shirttail hanging through his fly is a Senator, of course. He is for the moment the center of attention, displaying the gift which most politicians share: the ability to absorb infinite amounts of flattery.

There is one empty chair. That is reserved for the Director of the Office of Management and Budget. He is back at the office, having lost track of the time while poring over funding requests from the Bureau of Consumer Standards Enforcement.

. . .

It's time to say a little more about our hero, the wonk. He is pleasant and pleasing, not combative, and not so self-assertive that he would come off seeming ethnic (though in truth, as a child he was Italian). When he was in his mid-twenties and still a Capitol Hill staffer, he picked his specialty and in that way learned how to make himself useful. His wings were clipped a little by that decision (he had originally planned to specialize in foreign policy, which, *pace* the Council on Foreign Relations, is the policy problem of the leisure class). But his own selection has paid off anyway. If you plan to be in Washington for a lifetime, it's best to pick a groove.

Our wonk happened to pick the Congressional budget process as his specialty. He knows a lot about the budget reform act of 1974 and about rescission authority. He is perhaps a little too fond of facts and statistics, but he has a firm hold on his tiny sliver of opinion-making power. He considers himself an intellectual (in Washington, even a person who writes policy memos on tank-part procurement considers himself an intellectual).

Our wonk has a proposal, of course—all wonks do. His proposal, which he has hashed out in several articles and a book that sold 2,341 copies for the Free Press, involves restructuring the budget process, spreading the budget cycle out over four years, and making it more rational. If his plan were adopted, federal spending would be disciplined and flexible. The major decisions would all be made in an analytic, rational manner by disinterested wonks such as himself. I don't want to give the impression that the wonk thinks his proposal could actually be adopted. He is above all things realistic, and never zealous or utopian. Having come up with the reform is reward enough; imposing it upon the world would take too much zealotry. Like all wonks, his messianism is easygoing.

Our wonk happens to live in a very nice house near the

Cathedral in Northwest D.C. There are no novels around the house (he regrets the fact that he doesn't have time to read them), though you will find a few old copies of *Smithsonian* magazine, and maybe a few unopened issues of the *New York Review of Books*. The decor is colonial: nonideological American. There are nine-teenth-century prints of boats and water scenes on the walls. The furniture is not very expensive, but it is comfortable. The tele-vision and VCR are of top quality, allowing the wonk to tape "Nightline" without any distortion or snow. Our wonk even has a motto, typically self-ironic to fit in with the David Letterman era: "Ascending . . . Always Ascending."

This wonk is different from the wonks who preceded him. Earlier generations of wonks came to Washington and put pic-tures of the Roosevelts or John F. Kennedy on their walls. This wonk has a picture of James Schlesinger over his desk. The older generations quoted philosophers and utopians. This wonk quotes Peter Frampton lyrics. Like the rest of his generation, he is more ironic, less prone to idealism. On the other hand, his ambitions are loftier. Earlier generations of wonks merely dreamed of be-coming Secretary of State some day. Today's wonk dreams about becoming Secretary of State and then resigning to make $5 million a year as a consultant.

There's more money around Washington for this generation of wonks. An aide who writes a significant piece of legislation can then go into private industry and make millions of dollars circumventing it. On the other hand, the wonks of this genera-tion have missed out on living through historic events. In 1973, our wonk tried to start a riot when the vice-principal of his high school declared that students could no longer smoke during gym class. It was going to be very exciting, but instead of sending out the National Guard, the vice-principal dispatched a socially con-scious sociology teacher. He wore clogs and tried to persuade the rioters that what they should really be protesting was the use of paraquat over pot fields in Mexico.

In Washington, this generation of wonks will sit in nightclubs until the early morning hours, spilling buffalo-wing sauce on their red ties, complaining because their moment in the sun is so boring. The '60s produced the counterculture, the Vietnam syndrome, the welfare state, the drug culture. By the time this generation of wonks came to D.C., everything had already been screwed up. There was nothing left but to go and lead a soft, painless life, dragged along by the previous generation like a dinghy that bounces along behind a yacht.

The courses at the CRP dinner come with amazing rapidity. First a few slivers of salmon, then a green soup of some kind. The contemptuous waiters dribble leftovers onto the shoulders of unlucky diners. The dinner is breast of chicken with some yellow sauce on it, accompanied by morose asparagus. The dinner rolls will hold you until you can get home.

An orchestra plays the most banal big-band favorites ("Take the 'A' Train" tests the outer limits of its repertoire), though only the drums can be heard over the clanking silverware. Conversation consists of bartering information with your neighbor. Those who are not witty in Washington meet their conversational obligations by supplying inside information. The rumors, often wrong, are nonetheless always believed, because it is pleasant and exciting to believe them. The diners are always on the lookout for news that will lead to someone else's political ruin; often there is the haunting fear that a brewing scandal might be minor.

Nobody gets drunk at these dinners. If a wonk were to get drunk, he might get argumentative, or worse, philosophical. Even in the most plastered state, however, he would certainly not get lewd. Unlike dinners in New York and Los Angeles, there is no sexual tension lurking when wonks dine together. This is because wonks do not have sexual characteristics, since all of their erotic urges are channeled into perusals of the *Washington Post* op-ed page. The dinner conversation is thus not very animated. Nobody talks with his hands. As always, our wonk is engaged in an effort to steer the conversation back to his specialty, budget reform. Given that this is Washington, he is often successful. If someone is rude enough to mention art or fiction, a frosty silence settles over the table.

The rube from Dayton has trouble adjusting to all this. His wife does not say a word throughout the meal. But the roughest fit is the Senator. Having grown accustomed to the conversational style of the world's greatest deliberative body, the Senator naturally assumes that all dinner conversation revolves around fart jokes, ethnic jokes, blow-job jokes and tit jokes. The Senator does get drunk, even if it means tackling a waiter and insisting on extra bottles of wine for the table. Toward dessert, after his enunciations have lost some of their edge, the Senator deludes himself into the belief that he is thinking. This will lead to a series of long sentences that nobody else at the table will be able to follow.

Inevitably, conversation will settle on summer vacation plans. Wonks spend their winters dreaming of exotic summertime adventures in Bethany, Delaware. In Bethany, or in nearby Rehoboth, the wonk can spend a week lying on the beach reading a biography of George Kennan and persuade himself he is broadening his horizons. The wonk will not be distracted by any daring bathing suits. Well-behaved little wonk children will play quietly in the sand nearby. At night, a group of wonks will get together, have a light beer or two, and dine on barbecued swordfish while ridiculing the minority whip. If one of the wonks is a newspaper columnist, he will be busy with his obligatory here-I-am-on-vacation-and-how-trivial-all-the-problems-of-Washington-now-seem column. That done, he can go back to the discussion of redistricting possibilities still simmering in the kitchen.

Once during the week at the beach, the wonk and his friends will venture the twenty minutes south to Ocean City, where they can quiver before working-class bathers who wear string bikinis and monstrous tattoos. The wonks will walk warily past the pinball arcades, which are *so* loud and crowded, and then, having downed a milk shake or a taco, they'll return to the safety of the wonk enclave, feeling relieved to get out of the squalor.

It is hard to sustain a conversation on the virtues of Bethany for over three minutes. Thus, the entire table is relieved when the Director of the Council on Responsible Priorities taps on the microphone and signals the start of the tributes. A stream of Senators and prominent House leaders follows him to the podium, giant, booming men with large heads and good features, inflicting their bonhomie on their audience.

Finally, amidst a symphony of sycophancy, it is time to introduce the President. The director of the think tank does the honors. Unfortunately, his introduction becomes his own personal Vietnam. He launches into it with the best of intentions, but the further down he gets into his swamp of flattery, the more it becomes evident that there is no way he can extricate himself with honor. After the director gracelessly evacuates the podium, the band lets loose and the President mounts the stage. The President is brought to the podium. The audience, so happy to be in his presence, near the nut of power, is positively giddy at this point. They admire him, for he is a moderate man, a Beltway creature, courageously leading the American people to see the necessity of his own reelection.

The President starts with the two jokes that are obligatory at every Washington gathering. The first involves laying economists end to end, and the second is a reference to Everett Dirksen's remark about a few billion here and a few billion there. After the jokes, the President declares, "What I am about to say is not fashionable in these times." Then he proceeds to string together a few of the most fashionable truisms that have ever passed human lips.

He continues: "We have come upon a crucial moment in American history, probably the most dangerous yet exciting moment in human affairs. There are some who would counsel that we stick our heads in the sand." (This, of course, is an absolute lie—nobody ever counsels any such thing.) "Some would urge us to take rash, dangerous measures."

Having demolished his two straw men, the President boldly declares that he prefers a middle course. His speech drags somewhat, though, owing to the fact that the policy he is espousing lacks even a whiff of substance. There are a lot of sentences that begin, "We must . . . we must. . . ."

Then the President has an impulse of unfortunate charity. To share credit for the great work CPR has accomplished, he has decided to read out a list of the "foot soldiers" who made his administration possible. He asks people to stand when their names are read. A frenzy of mixed emotions sweeps the room. Everyone wants his name read, but nobody wants to actually stand up and perform this crass ritual of accepting glory. Politicians have no trouble playing out these vulgar dramas but do not understand that while wonks desperately seek glory, it is equally important that they not appear to seek it. As the names are read, however, a few of the honorees apparently feel no such embarrassment, and they rocket from their chairs, beaming unabashedly. Others make a more perfunctory effort, lifting their backsides a few millimeters from the seat as a nearby man slaps them on the back and a boisterous woman, infused with a pride of association, urges them, "Stand up." Our hero wonk merely smiles when his name is read.

The applause is perfunctory at first, but as more names are read, each member of the audience realizes that the chance of his own name passing from the President's lips is growing increasingly remote. The applause grows sharper; it acquires a brittle, envious tone. Finally, the last few names elicit nothing more than approving yelps from the people sitting at the honorees' table. The audience is now, for the most part, in a foul mood. Nobody is paying attention as the President finishes his speech with a rousing look into the bright future. There's some Reaganesque

City on the Hill rhetoric, and pretty soon the band is playing and he is out the door.

The end of the President's speech is like a starter's gun, for now the most important section of the evening has begun. The director of the think tanks gets up to officially bring the dinner to a close, but no one is listening. People are out of their chairs, darting quickly about the room, schmoozing and greeting. This is the dance of our democracy. Seen from overhead, it might look random, as people dart from greeting to greeting. But the patterns are set, as the wonks of all policy areas bound from contact to contact. Circulating, circulating. Our hero the wonk exchanges a hearty hello with a famous Soviet scholar. Then he's off with his arm around a prominent editor. A few seconds later he can be seen mingling with the Attorney General, and next he is chatting with a possible future employer across the room. Finally he gets to exchange a hello with the Treasury Secretary.

Circulating, circulating. A young apprentice wonk—a version of our own wonk as he appeared fifteen years ago—detains him and engages him in five minutes of profitless conversation. (Washington is the only town in America where the middle-aged have more fun.) Then there is the push to the chairman of his oversight subcommittee. Subcommittees are powerful; the wonk is even gracious to the Congressman's wife.

He's still circulating, circulating, and in heaven. This is the delicious mixture of work and play. This is what life is for, mingling and having access to the powerful. These happy snippets of conversation will keep him going for the next month of hard work, and then there will be another dinner, and maybe a higher stratum of wonks will seek him out. He's so happy that he spends a good fifteen minutes consoling a has-been whose nomination was shot down amidst much disgrace by a Senate confirmation committee.

Maybe, decades hence, he will no longer be a mere wonk. He will have become an institution, the way Henry Kissinger and Jeane Kirkpatrick are now. Every eye will be on him as he sits in a room. People will mention to their dinner mates, "Did you see that Frank Richards is here?" He will turn down appearances on "This Week with David Brinkley." He will have access to the oval office. He may even get to speak slowly.

At the peak of this circulating frenzy, someone grabs a microphone and has the band strike up "God Bless America." Influenced by the giddy drug of each other's presence, the audience sings it. The sight of all these healthy Americans, these handsome faces, so powerful, hardworking, virtuous, victorious, and on the inside, proudly belting out the simple song of love of nation—it is one of those rare moments when patriotism is sincerely felt. In tomorrow's edition, the *Washington Times* will write that there was an "electrifying" rendition of "God Bless America." The reporter from the *Washington Post* will note only that it was "sung loud."

What a magical night it has been!

A Farewell to Politics

Terry Teachout

I loved everyone, and everyone loved me—a great feeling for an unwanted child of abusive parents. When I got "home," I found I was pregnant. Aaron was born May 6, 1970. Now I work in a factory folding clothes. I find the world incredibly cold and cruel. All I have of beauty in my life is my son and my memory of those three days.

Carole Gray, *a Woodstock alumna,*
quoted in Rolling Stone

I was born in 1956, slightly past dead center of the baby boom, and received my high school diploma in 1974. A bit too young to have served in Vietnam, I was just old enough to drink deeply of the confusion of older boomers like Carole Gray of Columbus, Ohio, who went to Woodstock and got pregnant and lived miserably ever after.

I was fascinated by the '60s as a fly is fascinated by a spider. I let my small-town crewcut turn shaggy and went to see *Woodstock* and duped my unwitting parents into buying me a Fender bass. I decided that if the war lasted long enough, I would enroll as a conscientious objector. (I was too prim to contemplate moving to Canada.) I even sang a Bob Dylan song, "George Jackson," at a high school talent assembly, twelve-string guitar in hand, accompanied by a young man who, like me, ended up in New York, although he became a Democratic Socialists of America functionary while I went to work for the New York *Daily News*. To have done all of this in the course of growing up in a smallish Missouri town (pop. 20,000) seems to me worth recording, if not bragging about.

Whatever happened to the '60s, the decade that poor Carole Gray lived in, the decade with which I flirted so avidly? If you seek its monument, look no further. You just read it. Her sad memoir of Life After Woodstock sums up the '60s better than a three-volume novel. Most important, it captures an essential fact about the children of the '60s: faced at last with the realities of life, they promptly renounced their faith in politics as a way of changing those realities.

Renounced politics? The generation that took to the streets and disrupted Presidential conventions and burned its draft cards? The generation of *Make love, not war* and *Hey, hey, LBJ, how many kids did you kill today?* Absolutely. The children of the '60s, for all their talk of revolution, abdicated all thought of political responsibility. They did it in the name of principle, and they did it without hesitation.

How well I know the truth of those words. I majored in music in college. Like most of my peers, I assumed that my next stop was graduate school, a place that struck everyone I knew as an eminently suitable environment in which to live out the next act of our lives. I voted, but that was it. I played no role in campus politics and never took part in any kind of political campaign. The formative political experience of my youth was not Vietnam but Watergate. My birthright was cynicism. I was more or less conservative, at least to the extent that I distrusted big government, feared chaos, and read *National Review*. But I certainly wasn't prepared to do anything about it. I belonged to the party of Igor Stravinsky—and of Steely Dan. Politics was for older people (grownups, I suppose), not people like me. And most of the people I knew were, in this respect, exactly like me.

We took our cue from our older brothers and sisters, the children of the '60s, who drew from minimal experience the conclusion that politics was evil, that all politicians were dishonest, that the only way to live was for yourself alone. To be sure, they ate and slept "politics." They were endlessly concerned that their music be politically correct, that their diet be politically correct, that their clothes be politically correct. In the broadest sense of the word, they politicized everything they touched. But they knew nothing of real politics, politics in its earthiest and most meaningful sense: the act of running for office, or helping somebody else run for office, in order to effect policies that change people's lives. They sneered at the kind of politics that keeps the lights and water and welfare checks coming, that runs on handshakes and compromises and knowing people's first names.

For the boomers of the '60s, only one form of direct political action was permissible: protest. And even that limited involvement in the political sphere was construed as a special activity rather than an ongoing style of life. In the '60s, you spent one week a year marching on the Pentagon. The other fifty-one were spent mouthing revolutionary platitudes (most of them culled from album jackets) and concentrating on such purely personal matters as promiscuous coupling, illegal drugs, and rock and roll, three of the most profoundly self-centered pursuits devised by the mind of man.

Needless to say, the protest "movement" died out as soon as the Vietnam War ended and the proximate cause of rebellion was removed. (It also died out because it is easier to cut a class to go to a rally than it is to skip work.) Remember all those *Time* cover stories about how the baby boomers were going to transform politics in the '80s? Remember Jim Morrison snarling about how "they got the guns but we got the numbers"? Well, it was true.

We had the numbers—and we used them to help elect Ronald Reagan President, in case you were too busy listening to old Doors albums to notice. Not only that, our generation failed altogether to produce the young, vibrant Kennedy-type politicians who would change the world, or even a couple of Congressional districts. Remember Gary Hart? He wasn't in his thirties when he slipped on Donna Rice and disappeared down the memory hole. He was in his fifties.

In renouncing the everyday realities of party politics, the older baby boomers opted out of what should have been the most significant and divisive passions of their generation. Look back at 1960. Dwight Eisenhower had given way to John Kennedy, a man who, for all his undeniable weaknesses as a statesman, was the most viscerally exciting American politician since FDR. The civil rights movement was coming to a boil. Social scientists were beginning to tell us that government programs could eliminate poverty in America once and for all. The election of Kennedy was a quintessentially political moment, a time when what government did, or did not do, was a matter of intense interest to the average American, when there were most definitely two sides to every political question, when party affiliation was a matter of the utmost seriousness. And the children of the '60s, the baby boomers who were supposed to make the world over, didn't notice. The ones who got all the press were too busy protesting and taking drugs and having sex to dirty their hands with practical day-to-day politics; the ones who didn't get the press, who married early and built houses and started families, came in due course to the same cynical conclusions about the gaudy hopes of Camelot.

What happened? The line of eligibility for military service in Vietnam divides the baby boomers almost exactly in half. The older boomers, the ones who faced the dilemma of whether or not to serve in Vietnam, are the people you usually think about when you hear the term "baby boomers," and Vietnam seems to have broken them. They were the ones who lost their nerve and were never heard from again. Were they victims of the damage the war did to America's national self-image? Or was it that most of the boomers *didn't* serve in Vietnam, that an entire generation of spoiled middle-class brats never had to undergo any kind of testing experience at all? I can't tell you. But it's clear beyond question that the older boomers, whatever their reasons, simply gave up somewhere down the line.

Browsing through the Woodstock anniversary issue of *Rolling Stone*, I ran across another quote that caught my eye, this one from a fellow named Peter Tonks, who lives, not surprisingly, in Denver: "I have remained an alternative person. I do not own a Porsche, nor do I drink Perrier. I occasionally dig out old copies of *Rolling Stone* and wonder what happened." The conventional wisdom, of course, is that Peter Tonks and his fellow alternative people are going to wake up one day and discover that they have immense political power at their disposal, at which time they will begin to transform American society. Don't wait for it. Their entire background is apolitical; their deepest instincts are apolitical. They will never go very far beyond the mannerisms of protest acquired in their college days. They are more interested in scratching out a living, in writing novels and screenplays and songs—and in transforming the American academy, their one long-lasting (and, at least potentially, most destructive) achievement. The older boomers will be remembered as the generation that never realized its potential, political or otherwise. Like Bartleby the Scrivener, they preferred not to.

I understand the older boomers not merely because I partook of their ethos but because, in 1983, I turned my back on it. I returned to college that year in search of a more fulfilling career, a career move that is about as baby-boomish as you can get. I wanted to be, of all things, a psychotherapist. In the course of talking myself out of that mad pursuit, I noticed that something had changed—and that it wasn't me.

Having returned to college, I found myself surrounded by the children of the second half of the baby boom, the children who, born after 1956, knew only two Presidents: Jimmy Carter and Ronald Reagan. Vietnam meant nothing to them. They were untouched by the drift and indecision that had blighted the older boomers, the drift that seemed so eerily like the loss of will that paralyzed the British survivors of the First World War and led inexorably to the second one.

The first thing I noticed about the world these confident kids were making was the existence of a conservative newspaper on my campus. The success of the *Dartmouth Review* had spawned it, and a hundred others like it. The undergraduates who published this paper, I quickly realized, took politics very seriously indeed. Their paper existed solely to further political goals. (At first, in fact, it was the organ of the local chapter of Campus Republicans.) None of the students who put it out was headed for graduate school—unless you count law school. They were deeply disillusioned with the intellectual life of the university, which was dominated by tenured totalitarians whose cultural and political sympathies started on the left and went leftward from there. For them, the academy was hopeless, beyond changing. It was also irrelevant.

Reading that paper and talking to the students who published it caused me to realize that while the '60s had been about private lives, the '80s were about public ones. I had been hearing about yuppies, about people who cared only for food processors and Porsches, and now that I knew some of them I realized that they weren't like that at all. The younger boomers in whose midst I found myself were oriented toward doing, not thinking about what had to be done, much less the dangers of doing what had to be done. They ran their paper in a confrontational style and they conceived politics as a series of confrontations. Above all, they were *practical*. They wrote about the making and shaping of policy, precisely the kind of politics the older boomers had so devoutly shunned. They viewed their writing as a means to an end: the end of political power. And there was nothing futile or idealistic about their dreams of power. The President of the United States, after all, was a charter subscriber to *National Review*, and rumor had it that he was hiring people like me by the dozen.

I was not the first person who, confronted by the certainties of youth, felt the nagging itch of self-doubt. My apolitical brand of conservatism, the product of my fascination with the '60s, was looking more and more like a slightly absurd irrelevancy. I longed to be young, *really* young, once more. This was my chance. Shucking my wire-rimmed diffidence, I signed up for the staff of my campus paper and thereby joined the Reagan Revolution. Before I knew it, I was turning out snappy, sarcastic columns about the ideological sins of the official campus newspaper. I even learned enough about grantsmanship to help get our paper funded by a right-wing foundation.

It wasn't long before I abandoned my warm and fuzzy fantasy of becoming a psychotherapist and went off to seek my true destiny. Unfortunately, or so it seemed at the time, I got it wrong. I should have moved to Washington, D.C., and gotten a job cranking out policy papers for the Heritage Foundation or drafting speeches for some middle-level Reagan administration bureaucrat, like a thousand other ambitious young conservative journalists. Instead, I went to New York and became an assistant editor at a highbrow magazine. This detour was inadvertent. The magazine offered me a job and I took it, figuring that while New York wasn't Washington, it wasn't Kansas City, either.

Two years later, I moved over to the editorial page of the New York *Daily News* and began spending my waking hours parsing Supreme Court decisions. I had never written an editorial in my entire life. My only previous experience as a professional newspaperman had been as a part-time music critic for the *Kansas City Star*. But I learned. Teetering on the cusp of 1956, I had to choose. The boomers just older than me were busy listening to Philip Glass and reading Ann Beattie; the boomers just

younger than me were busy changing the world. I didn't want
to be left behind. So I switched sides.

In America, a mere half-dozen years can turn everything
you thought you knew inside out. The younger boomers, the
ones I first met in 1983, are still engaged—in a manner of speaking. But they are making their way in a rapidly changing environment, one in which the ordering principles of postwar
American politics have broken down.

Hard times have lately fallen on ideologues of all kinds, both
the tie-dyed stop-the-war kids and the angry right-wingers who
opposed them so passionately and whose opposition issued, a
decade after the fact, in the election of Ronald Reagan. The old
rallying points of both sides have since evaporated. The Berlin
Wall has fallen. The United States isn't at war with anybody.
The economy insists on staying in pretty good shape. Drugs
aren't fun anymore. With the exception of abortion (and, increasingly, affirmative action), nobody seems to want to get angry
about anything. Nor are there any particularly attractive poles
around which new political movements are coalescing. It is
highly unlikely that the anti-Communism of the '90s will be, say,
anti-Islam or anti-pollution.

We live in a queer political landscape today, and it is leading
to all sorts of peculiar behavior: strange bedfellows, unlikely
compromises, a distinct loss of ideological bite. The most striking
symptom of this sea change is the piece Francis Fukuyama published in *The National Interest* last year called "The End of History?" Fukuyama, at the time a highly placed State Department
policy analyst, argued that "history," by which he meant international ideological strife, had come to an end because liberal
democracy had triumphed throughout the world. I admire Fukuyama for catching the wave of political speculation; he'll
doubtless be remembered as the Charles Reich of the late '80s.
And I agree with him to this extent: there's something going on,

at least in America, that requires a long, cool look. But it's not the end of history. It's a weakening of America's postwar faith in the power of politics to make the world a significantly better place.

Part of this weakening, of course, is due to the political burning-out of the older baby boomers. But the boomers are not wholly responsible. Politics, as the Reagan Revolution taught me, is about policy, and there can be no impassioned debates about policy when the Russians are waving a white flag and the War on Poverty has been declared over and the welfare state commands the general allegiance of all Americans. Politics, moreover, is about reality, about the splitting of differences in pursuit of a reasonably common goal. But look at today's great "political" battle: the battle over abortion. How can this possibly be construed as a "political" question? It is, in fact, the least political of questions, and it is being "debated" in a frankly apolitical way. Instead of trying to find a patch of common ground, however small, both sides are arguing for the *removal* of the abortion problem from the realm of politics, for the general imposition of an absolutist position on the entire country. If abortion is in fact the hottest political question of the '90s, the fundamental issue that makes ordinary people choose sides, then we are undoubtedly headed for a profoundly apolitical period in American life, a period of open antinomianism, of single issues run amok; a period, too, when the older baby boomers, whatever side they choose, will know what to do (take to the streets) and will do it.

What about the younger boomers? They were the ones who caught the bug from Ronald Reagan. But exactly what was the bug they caught? Was it conviction? Or merely ambition? While the younger boomers were the rank and file of the Reagan Revolution, such as it was, it now seems clear that few of them had any particular use for the comprehensive ideology that older conservatives had so painstakingly worked out. What they sought was personal power. They changed nothing; instead, they became jobholding bureaucrats. Staunch supporters of Reaganomics and the free market, they coolly looked the other way when older hands reminded them of the conservative movement's traditional position on self-restraint and the inner check. "I love Ronald Reagan," a coke-snorting Washington speechwriter fresh out of college told me over a drink shortly after I moved to New York, "but I don't want him in my bedroom."

And what of their leader? It seems increasingly obvious to me that Ronald Reagan was the man who led America away from politics. His style and appeal were in every way antipolitical. Indeed, he ran *against* politics, and won by a landslide. True, he called himself a conservative, and we knew in our hearts that it was so. (Did he not say all the right things and quote all the right people and hire all the good guys?) But Reagan's was a conservatism without tears. He taught an entire generation of youthful politicians, Republicans and Democrats alike, to accept things as they are, to give away anything rather than risk the fatal hemorrhage of power. True, Reagan brought the conservative movement into the tent of politics. But in so doing, he dulled the cutting intellectual edge of the movement by giving it real power for the first time in its short life. Surely it is no accident that at the beginning of the Reagan years, the most influential and widely discussed book on the right was George Gilder's *Wealth and Poverty*, a political and economic tract for the times that presented with infectious passion the case for the transforming power of the conservative vision; and that at the end, the most influential and widely discussed book on the right was Tom Wolfe's *The Bonfire of the Vanities*, a novel *(a novel!)* that demonstrated with infectious relish how little effect that vision had had on the daily realities of political life in America's greatest city.

To mention *The Bonfire of the Vanities* is to be forcibly reminded that racial tensions appear to be on the rise in America. To the extent that this is true, it is because blacks (and, to a somewhat lesser degree, Hispanics) continue to cling desperately to their faith in the power of politics. This is understandable, since it was through politics that blacks won the great civil-rights battles of the '60s. But the tried-and-true methods of the '60s no longer work. Preferential policies aimed at improving the lot of the black community have reached the point of diminishing returns; some of them, particularly affirmative action, are making life worse for the very people they are meant to help. Therein lies the problem. Black political leaders clamor for more and better help from the government. The rest of the country (including, one suspects, many middle-class blacks) views the clamor as an exercise in greedy irrelevance. It's a recipe for impotent rage, for full-scale demagoguery from bigots of every hue.

The baby boomers know exactly how destructive affirmative action is, for they see its consequences at first hand: they are the middle managers forced to carry the ball for aging, high-minded executives who continue to wrestle with liberal guilt. As one Democratic pollster who studies middle-class attitudes recently noted: "There is no debate on affirmative action. Everybody is against it. . . . It's a paradox that the Democratic Party takes it as an accepted principle whereas the base we need to reach in order to win elections takes it as a conventional wisdom that it is an injustice to the middle class." Substitute "blacks" for "the Democratic Party" and "baby boomers" for "the middle class" and the second great political dilemma of the '90s emerges in stark relief.

If politics in the '90s is headed for trouble, what about ideology? That glorious millennium, the end of ideology, has been predicted at roughly ten-year intervals, as David Brooks pointed out in *The Wall Street Journal* last year, and the prophets are at it again. They are, as always, wrong. Two centuries after the fact, the citizens of the West continue to take their places in two endless files, one descending from Burke, the other from Rousseau. Ideology is still alive and well, even among the baby boomers.

But how will the boomers manifest their ideology? What will they fight over? The whole point of ideology, after all, is that it must eventually lead to battle. Even the pathetic children of the '60s did battle; they chose the wrong battlegrounds, and they gave up in apathy and despair, but they fought as long as they could see the point of it. Similarly, the younger boomers will continue to fight for what they believe in. But in the absence of fundamental divisions of the electorate over questions of public policy, I suspect that the great battles of the '90s will be fought in another arena: that of culture.

By "culture" I mean to cast a very broad net. Abortion is a good example. So is "family policy." These are pseudopolitical issues that are more deeply rooted in the way we live, and the way we feel we (and others) ought to live, than the way we vote. The halls of Congress will resound with clamorous quarrels over what the government should do about day care; blood will be shed in the streets over what the government should do about abortion. But these fights will not be about political differences so much as they will be about cultural differences. When *The New Republic*, inventor of the Zeitgeist Checklist, finds it prudent and appropriate to run a cover story singing the praises of gay marriage, it isn't really talking about passing a bill. Nobody's going to write that kind of bill into law. What *The New Republic* is suggesting is that it's time for the articulate class to stop arguing about public policies and start arguing about the private and personal convictions that underlie those policies.

I refer also to the "culture" of the American academy. Though the astonishing success of Allan Bloom's book *The Closing of the American Mind* has been chewed over endlessly in the media, that doesn't make it any less interesting. It was Bloom who first brought home to the general public the fact that ferocious guerrilla warfare is being waged in the groves of academe by that handful of '60s refugees who cared enough about their left-wing ideas to hide out in America's colleges and universities, there to continue their savage attacks on tradition and order. As for secondary education, it's impossible to ignore the growing new movement that aggressively advocates a restoration of "content" and "values" in the public schools, though it may ultimately manifest itself in the private (and privatized) schools that will dominate this country's academic life after the coming breakup of America's common school system.

Finally, I mean "culture" in its most familiar sense: the fine arts. The '60s were a time of hideous, inconceivable disaster in the arts. Every medium was brutally despoiled in its turn; the aftermath was postmodernism, a style born of stunned shock and devoted to cynical clowning about the things that matter most. Postmodernism, in its various forms, has become the *lingua franca* of American art. But the younger boomers, increasingly sick of the bad art that is so large a part of the legacy of the '60s, have begun at last to reject it. That Tom Wolfe, by writing an utterly old-fashioned social novel, should have excited and galvanized younger baby boom intellectuals more than any other writer of the late '80s seems to me to be the most startling indication of things to come in the culture of the '90s.

The younger boomers, then, having escaped the effects of Vietnam and the excesses of the '60s, will lead the charges in the culture wars of the '90s. But they will not do so as part of mass political movements, and least of all as part of a revived conservative movement. The salad days of Reaganism are over. It is not merely that "culture" is a less effective rallying point than "politics"; it is that there is no true consensus among the younger boomers (or the post-boomers) over what the right cultural values should be. Some of the younger boomers are traditionalists who have staked out the high ground of nuclear families and religious orthodoxy. But many others, "liberal" and "conservative" alike, have been significantly influenced by the loosened morality of the '60s. Not long after I moved to New York, I found myself looking for an articulate young woman who could state the case against legalized abortion for a magazine article on which I was working. I called up a friend of mine in Washington,

a well-placed fellow who knew his way around all the right net-
works, and asked for some names. "There aren't any," he told
me grimly. "Not in Washington, anyway. The women here say
what they have to say, but they don't believe a word of it. If they
had to choose between a baby and a better job, they'd take the
job every time."

Any movement divided that deeply is no longer a movement. It is a shaky coalition on the verge of realignment. And
there can be little doubt that we are about to see a drastic realignment of the ideological patterns that have dominated American
public life since the end of the Second World War, a transfor-
mation as great and profound as the one that ushered in the
beginning of modern liberalism at the turn of the century. The
survivors may still call themselves liberals and conservatives;
they will almost certainly call themselves Democrats and Republicans. But they will be operating in terms of a new ideological
reality: a post-'60s reality and, for the baby boomers, a postpo-
litical reality.

A society that feeds voraciously on politics is headed for a
very great fall. America took just such a fall in the '60s, a fall
from which it is only now recovering. But Americans have historically preferred to take their politics with a very large grain of
salt, and it strikes me that in the wake of Ronald Reagan, we are
finally beginning to return to our normal, time-honored course,
one in which the average citizen is content to go about the business of living his private life, leaving politics to the professionals
who have chosen it as a vocation. Surely that will be good for
everybody, and not least for the conservative movement, which
has been delivered by the stony indifference of George Bush
from the corrupting temptation of political power and which can
now return to debating first causes, the proper role of any intellectual movement, be it of the left or of the right.

Those of us who fitted ourselves out in the early years of

Reaganism with the shields and swords of practical politics will thus be left with two possibilities: either find another suit of armor or go off to join our older brothers and sisters, the ones who remained alternative people, who proudly flaunt the fact that they do not own Porsches and do not drink Perrier, who light up their after-dinner joints and dig out old copies of *Rolling Stone* and wonder what happened.

As for me, I don't plan to sit in my living room sipping a Coors, leafing through old copies of *National Review* and wondering what happened. I know what happened, and I'm glad that it happened. I'm relieved to be able to say a not-so-fond farewell to politics, a business I never quite managed to feel at home in, a dark room whose light switches I couldn't find. In the end, I turned out to be a child of the '60s after all; it was culture that I cared about, not politics. The battles of the coming decade are the battles I long to fight, the battles over the latest novels and the newest symphonies and the curriculum at the neighborhood high school—and, yes, over whether or not abortion is (a) murder, (b) a woman's right to choose, (c) both, or (d) none of the above.

I still write editorials for a living, and I mean to do so for some time to come. It's a good job, and I don't care to fall off the ladder of professional success now that I've become something of a yuppie. Besides, I find that *local* politics, the nuts-and-bolts kind, has begun to engage my interest, a sure sign of advancing age. But it is, after all, only a job, and so I don't get overly worked up anymore, at least not from nine to five, about campaign financing and welfare reform and *perestroika*.

Instead, I go home after work and sit up late writing about Jerome Robbins and Jascha Heifetz and H. L. Mencken and rap music and how the academy is going to hell. I wax passionate as I stare at the green screen of my word processor and think about the things that matter to me. This is where I came in. A stopped clock, they say, is right twice a day. I think my second time to be right has just arrived.

NOTES ON CONTRIBUTORS

BRUCE BAWER contributes literary criticism to *The New Criterion* and *The American Scholar*, reviews books for *The Wall Street Journal*, and has published poems in *The Paris Review*, *Poetry*, *The Hudson Review*, and other journals. His books include *Diminishing Fictions: Essays on the Modern American Novel and Its Critics*. He is a director of the National Book Critics Circle.

RICHARD BROOKHISER is a senior editor of *National Review* and a columnist for the *New York Observer*. He is the author of *The Outside Story: How Democrats and Republicans Reelected Reagan* and the forthcoming *The Way of the WASP: How It Made America and How It Can Save It, So to Speak*.

DAVID BROOKS, formerly a Washington policy wonk, is now an editorial writer with *The Wall Street Journal*.

ANDREW FERGUSON is an editorial writer for the Scripps Howard News Service. He was assistant managing editor of *The American Spectator* from 1985 to 1989.

MAGGIE GALLAGHER is the author of *Enemies of Eros: How the Sexual Revolution Is Killing Family, Marriage and Sex and What We Can Do About It*. She is managing editor of *NY: The City Journal*, a journal of New York policy and politics published by the Manhattan Institute.

Prior to becoming a free-lance writer, GEORGE SIM JOHNSTON was a vice-president in the Corporate Finance Department of Salomon Brothers. His work appears in *Commentary*, *National Review*, *The American Spectator*, the *National Catholic Register*, and *Crisis*. He is at work on a novel about Wall Street in the early '80s.

ROGER KIMBALL is managing editor of *The New Criterion*. His work appears in the London *Times Literary Supplement*, *The Wall Street Journal*, *Architectural Record*, *Commentary*, *The American Scholar*, and *The New York Times Book Review*. He is the author of *Tenured Radicals: How Politics Has Corrupted Higher Education*.

DANA MACK teaches piano and writes about music for *The New Criterion*.

WALTER OLSON is a senior fellow at the Manhattan Institute. His work appears in *Fortune*, *Barron's*, and *The Wall Street Journal*. He is the author of the forthcoming *The Litigation Explosion*.

JOHN PODHORETZ is assistant managing editor of the *Washington Times*.

DONNA RIFKIND writes for *The Wall Street Journal*, the London *Times Literary Supplement*, *Commentary*, *The New Criterion*, and other publications.

LISA SCHIFFREN is Special Assistant to the Assistant Secretary of Defense for Special Operations/Low-Intensity Conflict. She spent much of 1988 and 1989 in Pakistan and Afghanistan gathering material for a book she is now writing. From 1984 to 1988 she wrote editorials and covered politics for the *Detroit News*. The views expressed in her essay are her own and do not necessarily reflect those of the Defense Department.

TERRY TEACHOUT is a member of the editorial board of the New York *Daily News.* His work appears in *The American Scholar, The American Spectator, Commentary, Musical America, National Review, The New Criterion, The New Dance Review,* and *The New York Times Book Review.* He is the editor of *Ghosts on the Roof: Selected Journalism of Whittaker Chambers, 1931–1959.*

RICHARD VIGILANTE is editor of *NY: The City Journal.*

SUSAN VIGILANTE is at work on her first novel.

ACKNOWLEDGMENTS

On behalf of the fifteen contributors to *Beyond the Boom*, I grate-fully acknowledge the steadfast support of Elaine Pfefferblit of Poseidon Press, and Glen Hartley and Lynn Chu, our agents for this book. They deserve as much credit for thinking of *Beyond the Boom* as I do; they put up with even more nonsense than I did in order to get it written and edited. In addition, we all owe Tom Wolfe a great deal more than his introduction to this book.

My personal thanks to Andrew Ferguson and Maggie Gal-lagher, who edited my contributions to *Beyond the Boom;* Bill Hammett of the Manhattan Institute, who has generously pro-vided a meeting place for the Vile Body from its early days onward; Midge Decter, confidante of more baby boomers, this one included, than anyone I know; George Sim Johnston, with-out whom the Vile Body would have remained nothing more than a good idea; Jonathan Cohen, Phil Marcus, Jim Capua, and Lewis H. Lapham, without whom I would probably still be living in Urbana, Illinois, studying psychology and wondering what New York was like; and Elizabeth Teachout, for reasons that (to lift a line from Kaufman and Hart) are nobody's business.